PIG TALES

PIG TALES

Kate Tym

Illustrated by John Blackman

SHAFTESBURY, DORSET · BOSTON, MASSACHUSETTS · MELBOURNE, VICTORIA

For Sue and Jem – perfect piggy pals!

First published in Great Britain in 1999 by
Element Children's Books
Shaftesbury, Dorset SP7 8BP

Published in the USA in 1999 by
Element Books, Inc.
160 North Washington Street,
Boston MA 02114

Published in Australia in 1999 by
Element Books and distributed by
Penguin Australia Limited,
487 Maroondah Highway, Ringwood,
Victoria 3134

Cover design by Mandy Sherliker.
Designed and typeset by Dorchester Typesetting Group Ltd.
Printed and bound in Great Britain by J.W. Arrowsmith Ltd.

British Library Cataloguing in Publication data available.
Library of Congress Cataloging in Publication data available.

ISBN 1 902618 50 5

Introduction

Last year my sister Sue, and her boyfriend, Jem, gave me a piggy calendar for Christmas. It was my dream gift; 365 days of lovely piggies beaming at me as I did the dishes. Twelve different porkers to keep me company as I pottered around my kitchen.

There's nothing like a wet snout and some big, leathery ears to get my heart fluttering and now I could experience that sensation every day of the year in the comfort of my own home! And, through *Pig Tales*, you'll be able to do the same – learning something of how people and their animals get along together and the wonderful ways that animals and humans show their mutual love. From life-saving porkers to gentle tales of pets enriching their family's lives *Pig Tales* has got something for everyone who's ever seen an animal and couldn't resist saying "*ahhh!*"

Over a year has passed since I got my calendar and I must admit as December 1998 approached I felt rather sad at the prospect of having to say goodbye to my lovely piggy pin-ups. But, luckily for me, Sue and Jem saved the day and bought me another piggy calendar to get me through to the next millennium!

Kate Tym

In Praise of a Pig

A pig is a jolly companion,
Boar, sow, barrow, or gilt –
A pig is a pal, who'll boost your morale,
Though mountains may topple and tilt.
When they've blackballed, bamboozled, and burned you,
When they've turned on you, Tory and Whig,
Though you may be thrown over by Tabby and Rover,
You'll never go wrong with a pig, a pig,
You'll never go wrong with a pig!

From *Gravity's Rainbow* by Thomas Pynchon

LuLu to the Rescue

WHEN Mr. and Mrs. Altsman of Beaver Falls bought their daughter, Jackie, a pot-bellied pig as a birthday present, little did they know that what they had actually got was a full-scale life saver. But LuLu the pig was exactly that.

It was August 1997 and Jo Ann and Jack Altsman were on vacation on Presque Isle in their vacation trailer. They'd taken their dog Bear (an American Eskimo dog) and . . . LuLu the pig. Their daughter had gone on vacation too and had left the Altsman's piggy sitting. As it turned out, having LuLu with them was just about the best thing that could have happened.

It was a lovely day, and Jack Altsman had decided to make the most of it by going off fishing on Lake Erie; Jo Ann meanwhile was relaxing in their trailer. Then, something terrible happened, Jo Ann suffered terrible pains in her chest and realized to her horror that she was having a heart attack! She lay, unable to move, on the floor of the trailer. Bear began barking frantically, but remained rooted to the spot, not knowing what to do to help his poor owner. But LuLu wasn't so slow, she took one look at Mrs. Altsman lying on the floor and she knew just what she had to do.

LuLu squeezed herself through the dog/pig flap and headed for the road. Normally LuLu didn't leave the little enclosure around the trailer without being attached to a leash, so heading out on her own was a very brave thing for the perky porker to do. LuLu stood patiently at the side of the road waiting for a car to come by, and when one did . . . she walked right out in front of it and lay down. Several people were

stopped in this way but not being as smart as LuLu they didn't understand what she was after, and as soon as she got up to lead them back to the trailer, they drove away.

Poor LuLu kept trotting back and forth to check on Mrs. Altsman, each time returning to her roadside vigil hoping to find someone to help her out. Finally, her patience paid off. A car approached, LuLu lay down, and the person driving it got out and followed as she squealed her way to the Altsman's trailer. He only followed her because he wanted to alert whoever owned her to the fact that their pig was in distress. But what he found when he got to the Altsman's trailer was that Jo Ann was in distress too! The unknown man rushed to call an ambulance and soon Mrs. Altsman was out of the trailer on her way to hospital for emergency heart surgery. Caring LuLu didn't even want to leave her then, and it was only after some firm words from the medics that she stopped trying to climb into the ambulance alongside Jo Ann!

LuLu had saved Mrs. Altsman's life. The medical staff told Jo Ann that if she'd had to wait only fifteen minutes longer for help to arrive she might well not have made it! And as for LuLu, the 150 pound pig was so determined to fetch help that she'd even risked cutting her own tummy when she'd squeezed herself back and forth through the doggy-sized door. But it was worth it in the end because not only did she get her loving owner back in one piece, but she got a delicious jelly donut as a reward too!

Who said that...?

"...all cry and no wool."

Samuel Butler on the merits of a pig.

Piggy History

40 million BC Archaeologists believe this is when the first pigs appeared on Earth.

7000 BC The pig was one of the first animals to be domesticated or trained by man.

4000 BC A royal decree from the Emperor of China made it law for the Chinese people to raise and breed pigs. The ancient Chinese often felt so attached to their herds that when they died they would sometimes even be buried with them!

4000-3000 BC	Egyptian hieroglyphics (picture writing) show that pigs were revered and were only eaten once a year.
1493 AD	Christopher Columbus – following orders from Queen Isabella of Spain sets off to the New World with a cargo of prize porkers. That's where North America's pig population comes from.
1539 AD	Hernando de Soto brings more pigs to North America – 15 in total. When he died three years later his 700 strong herd was sold – you guessed it – they all came from the first 15!
1760s	George Washington imports special hogs to establish breeding herds in the US.
1863	The city of Cincinnati, Ohio, was nicknamed Porkopolis as its pig business was so big.
1933	The year of the heaviest hog in history. His name was Big Bill and he was a Poland China pig who weighed in at a staggering 2,552 pounds – wow, that's some pig!
1980s	Pot-bellied pigs as pets come into vogue.
1999	*Pig Tales* published to critical acclaim!!

Did you know...?

According to scientists, pigs are total brainiacs –

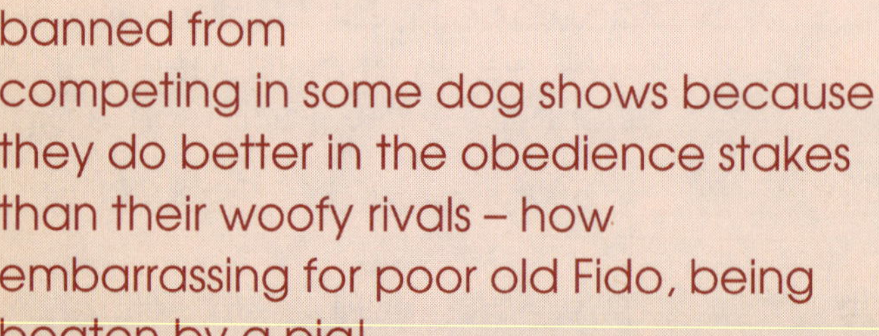

they're cleverer than dogs, cows, and even dolphins! Like real-life "Babes" in the US they're already banned from competing in some dog shows because they do better in the obedience stakes than their woofy rivals – how embarrassing for poor old Fido, being beaten by a pig!

Courageous Creatures

PIGS, a sanctuary, is a wonderful place. Set in the Eastern Panhandle of West Virginia, overlooking the Blue Ridge Mountains, the farm is 54 acres of rolling hills, pastures, and woods. There is an old two-storey farm house, and a new wood fence runs right up the long driveway. PIGS is home to around 350 pigs as well as miniature goats and sheep, a miniature horse, two miniature donkeys, three peacocks, chickens, turkeys, ducks, dogs and cats and even an emu! All the animals are there for rehabilitation having been rescued from sorry circumstances, and all of them are given a new start in life that enables them to forget their past traumas and start looking forward to a safe and secure future.

One of the pigs lucky enough to live there is a friendly fellow called Pork Chop. Pork Chop was living in the back yard of a family who lived in a trailer. He had very little shelter (only a tarpaulin wrapped around a tree) and spent most of his time exposed to whatever wind and rain was whistling around him. It wasn't a very nice life for him, and it was about to get much worse. The people who owned him didn't deserve the gift of such a lovely pig; they treated him badly and were only interested in the money they could make through using him for breeding. They were cruel people and on one terrible day the owner hit Pork Chop across the back with a heavy board as a way of disciplining him. Pork Chop's spine was fractured and he lost the use of his back legs. Fortunately he ended up in the caring hands of the people at PIGS, a sanctuary. When their vet saw the poor pig he said, "You are going to put him down, aren't you?" but luckily for Pork Chop it's Sanctuary policy to give an animal a chance at a quality life. It's only if they feel they really can't give an animal any sort of quality of life or if an animal will simply continue suffering that they will make the decision to have an animal put to sleep and end their misery. But with Pork Chop, they didn't feel this was the case. OK, so he couldn't walk, but he could do just about everything else that a pig might want to do!

He dragged himself around using his front legs, and his butt and back legs simply followed on behind. He had the best in food, vet care, and housing and he was just about as happy as a pig could be. He was a good-natured pig and anyone who visited the sanctuary simply fell in love with the pig who couldn't walk. People accepted him how he was and never dreamed he would ever be any other way.

Then, after about five years at PIGS, something truly amazing happened. It was a warm spring day and Pork Chop came out of his house (a small cabin with a disabled ramp built specifically for PIGS' disabled residents!) and . . . he was walking! He wasn't dragging his back legs behind him but was actually walking around on them! It was a real miracle. It seemed that the nerve endings in his spine, after all those years, had begun to repair themselves giving Pork Chop some feeling back in his hindquarters. Now Pork Chop never drags his back end to get around. Although he doesn't walk straight (he has to carefully position himself to stay up) he walks everywhere he wants to go. It seems the people at PIGS were absolutely right when they turned the vet's offer down – with time they were able to offer him everything a pig needs . . . including the chance to walk again!

Pork Chop is of course not the only pig to have found a loving home at PIGS. Heidi Ho is a feisty little pig who also had a tough start in life, but who has spent her later years making up for her bad beginning. Heidi Ho hadn't been properly trained when she was sold at just a few weeks old and her new owners didn't really know how to cope with her. One day, she ran away and her owners couldn't catch her. While running through the town in a panicked state, she was attacked by some dogs – she still has the scars on her neck to prove it. The situation was getting dangerous and the owners decided to call in animal control officers to see if they could catch their pig before any more harm could befall her. In order to stop the little creature they decided they would use a tranquilizer dart, but not being used to catching pigs they didn't really know which size dart to use and unfortunately they picked the wrong size for her little body. The dart penetrated her spine and shattered the vertebrae where the nerve endings come off.

Unlike Pork Chop, Heidi Ho will never walk on her back legs again.

PIGS got Heidi Ho from the animal control facility. She has lived at the sanctuary for two years and is affectionately referred to as "The Pig Who Can." Heidi Ho does everything the other pigs do except walk on all fours and run. She digs holes, rolls in the mud, drags herself across the yard to get to whatever she wants and her whole personality is: Don't feel sorry for me, I can do anything I want.

Heidi Ho is a small black pot-bellied pig and is an inspiration to all who get to know her. She truly doesn't believe she's disabled. Her best friends are Phyllis Louise (Weezer) and Pork Chop. Every night during the warm months, Heidi Ho will drag herself to the disabled cabin and sit in front of the ramp and wait for Jim Brewer (one of the Sanctuary's founders) to come and lift up her back end to get her started up the ramp to the entrance of the cabin. Once inside, she makes herself a nest in the hay and calls it a day. In the mornings, she comes down the ramp and is usually by the feed barn waiting for Dale (Jim's co-founder) and Jim to get outside to feed everyone. Jim says, "She is a true blessing – a pig with a winning, charming attitude." Hooray for Heidi Ho!

If you'd like more information about PIGS, a Sanctuary, here's their address:

Jim Brewer / Dale Riffle, Co-Founders, PIGS, a Sanctuary, PO Box 629, Charles Town, WV25414, USA

Web site address: www.pigs.org

Email: pigsanct@aol.com

Pen a pig

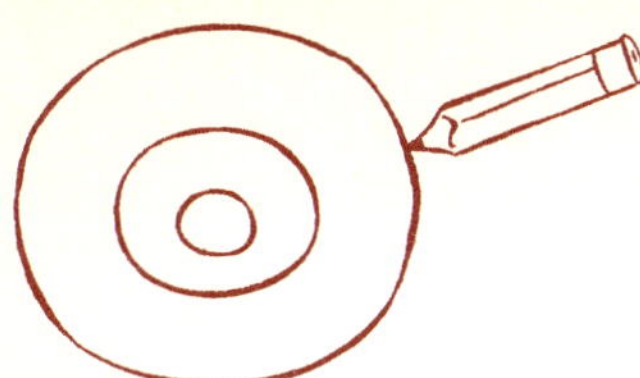

Easy peasy piggy penmanship.

First draw three circles . . .

Then add two triangles . . .

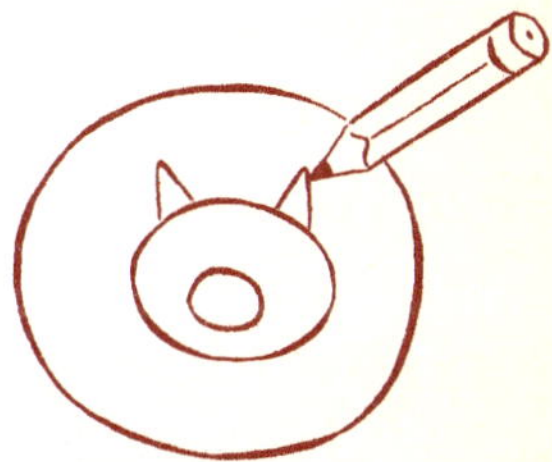

Now four dots . . .

Four lines for legs . . .

And one curly tail . . .

Cute pig!

Tiger-sized Love

Imagine patting a tiger on the head or taking one for a walk. Well, if you become a

tiger-sponsor at the special Petting Farm in Davidsonville, Maryland, that could be just what you'd be able to do. The tiger Sponsorship Program is part of the non-profit National Endangered Wild Animal Research and Conservation Center (NEWARCC) which was founded to inspire children and grown-ups to respect, protect, and preserve wildlife, the environment, and farmland. It's a sad fact that any wild animal has to live in captivity for its own safety and for human education, but ideally centers such as this one will help to ensure that in the future, all tigers can roam free just as nature intended.

For as little as $100, people can join the program of sponsorship and receive tiger viewing and petting privileges that are not open to other visitors to the farm. Tiffany and Tasha the two tigers seem more than happy to interact with their new human friends. They initially grew up as part of the Collinson family (Debbie Collinson founded the petting farm in 1990) but after about a year they were a bit too big for the house so they moved into the back garden and a special enclosure where they still receive lots of love, attention, and play time. Because Debbie didn't want the tigers to be handled all day long she restricted the petting to people who join the scheme, that way the tigers get lots of love without being pawed by people to the extent that they get a bit fed up with it. It seems Tiffany and Tasha, like their smaller cousins, have quite distinct characters and if either of them isn't in the mood for human kindness, they'll simply refuse to come down from their tree-top perches. But apparently Tiffany usually finds it quite hard to resist a scratch behind the ear and will come and put her enormous head right up against the enclosure wires to ensure maximum contact. And as for the people! They love it. Some people come back week after week, some once a month, and one lady, Gloria Nelson, now happily pays $100 a year to sponsor four wild Siberian tigers in Russia in an attempt to keep the species going. Apparently, there's nothing in the world like making a tiger purr and Collinson says that the tigers even make growly woofy sounds when they're enjoying themselves! Thrills don't come much bigger than that!

If you would like to know more about the NEWARCC sponsorship scheme you can contact them through their website at: **http://annap.infi.net/~newarcc/tigspon1.html**

Did you know...?

The pig was held sacred by the ancient Cretans because Jupiter was suckled by a sow!

Popular Piggies

Porky Pig

Porky Pig was the first Warner Bros. character to gain star status in the late 1930s. He made his screen debut in 1935 with a role in a film called "I Haven't Got a Hat." He was so fabulous that he soon progressed to a solo role in 1936.

Porky's diminutive stature and retiring personality made him the perfect foil for some of the brasher characters and he was often teamed up with big and bold Bugs Bunny and self-obsessed Daffy Duck. He was so popular that in 1943 he was even nominated for an Academy Award for his role in "The Swooner Grooner."

Porky's probably best known for his stammering catchphrase, "The-the-the-the-that's all folks!"

Pig parade

In April 1996 Liverpool University hosted Britain's first ever pet pig show! With pigs becoming more popular as pets they were able to muster some pretty stiff competition.

The piggy competitors were judged not just on their stunning good looks but on their level of obedience and particular talents too! One clever little porker could even play a musical instrument. I think he'd definitely get my vote!

Are You an Animal Worker or Shirker?

Section One
Have you ever:

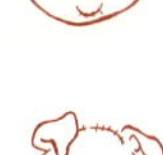

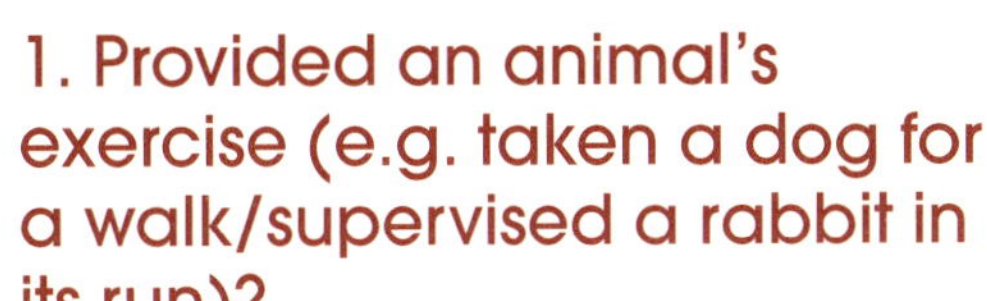

1. Provided an animal's exercise (e.g. taken a dog for a walk/supervised a rabbit in its run)?

A. Yes lots B. No Never
C. Once or twice

2. Given an animal its food?

A. Yes loads of times B. No
Never C. Once or twice

3. Groomed an animal (e.g. cleaned and brushed its coat)?

A. Yes loads of times B. No
Never C. Once or twice

4. Raised money for an animal charity?

A. Yes loads of times B. No
Never C. Once or twice

Answers Section One

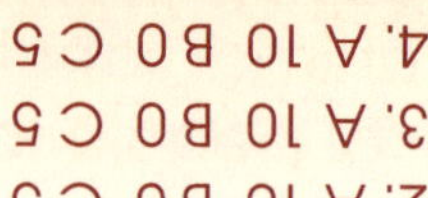

Make a note of your Section One score here ☐

Section Two

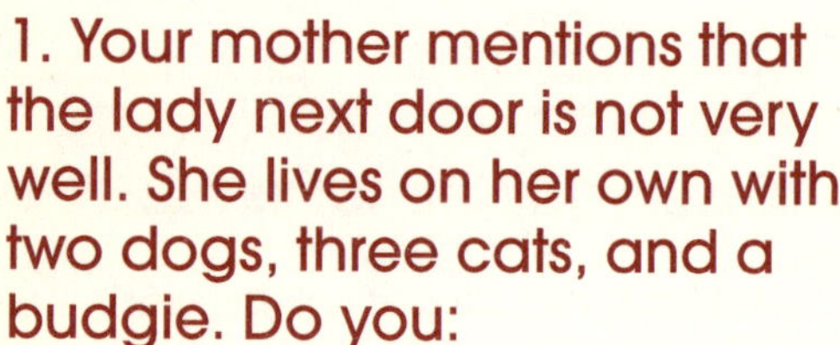

1. Your mother mentions that the lady next door is not very well. She lives on her own with two dogs, three cats, and a budgie. Do you:

A. Rush next door and offer to help take care of her animals for her until she's feeling better?

B. Rush next door to see if there's anything you can do for her and see if she would also like any help with her pets?

C. Say "Oh that's a shame" and go back to watching TV?

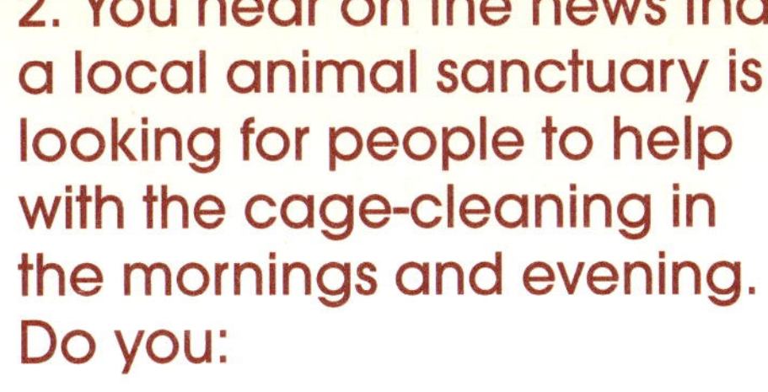

2. You hear on the news that a local animal sanctuary is looking for people to help with the cage-cleaning in the mornings and evening. Do you:

A. Go around and offer your services but secretly think that you'll be able to get off cage-cleaning duty pretty quickly and get on to something more fun – like grooming and stroking duty – real soon!?

B. Rush over and start helping with the cage-cleaning right away? If it makes the animals happy then it makes you happy too?

C. Forget about it – there's no way you're getting your hands dirty first thing in the morning?

3. Do you think zoos are:

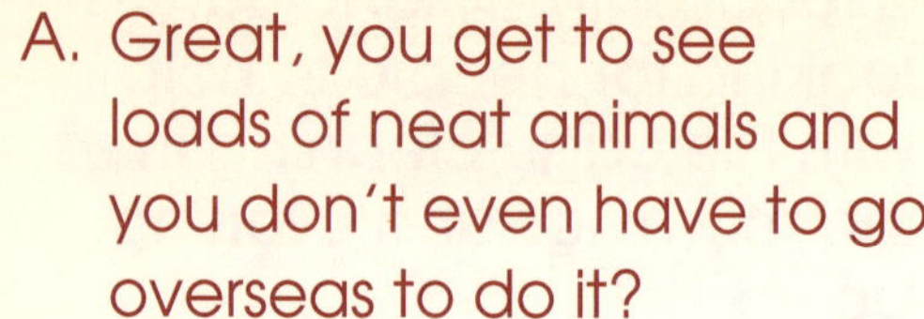

A. Great, you get to see loads of neat animals and you don't even have to go overseas to do it?

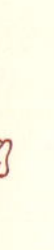
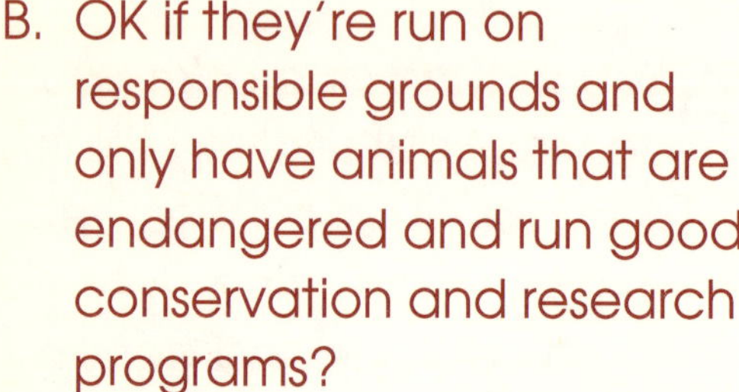

B. OK if they're run on responsible grounds and only have animals that are endangered and run good conservation and research programs?

C. Horrible – you don't want any animals to be locked up ever?!

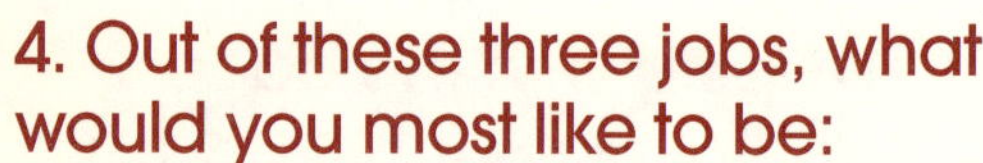

4. Out of these three jobs, what would you most like to be:

A. A wildlife photographer, seeing all those animals in their natural habitat without them even knowing you were there would be such a thrill?

B. The director of an animal sanctuary – helping animals back to health

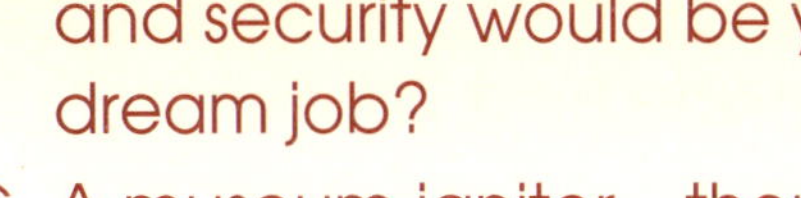

and security would be your dream job?

C. A museum janitor – then the only animals you'd have to look after would be stuffed ones?

5. Do you believe that most animals are intelligent, thinking, feeling beings?

A. No way – a bunny's a real dummy and I know how stupid my dog is?!

B. Yes – all animals are intelligent and have feelings just like you and me?

C. Yes – some animals are pretty smart but some aren't but they probably all feel something?

6. When you meet an animal for the first time do you?

A. Take your time, talk quietly, and let the animal get to know you before you really go for the love and hugs?

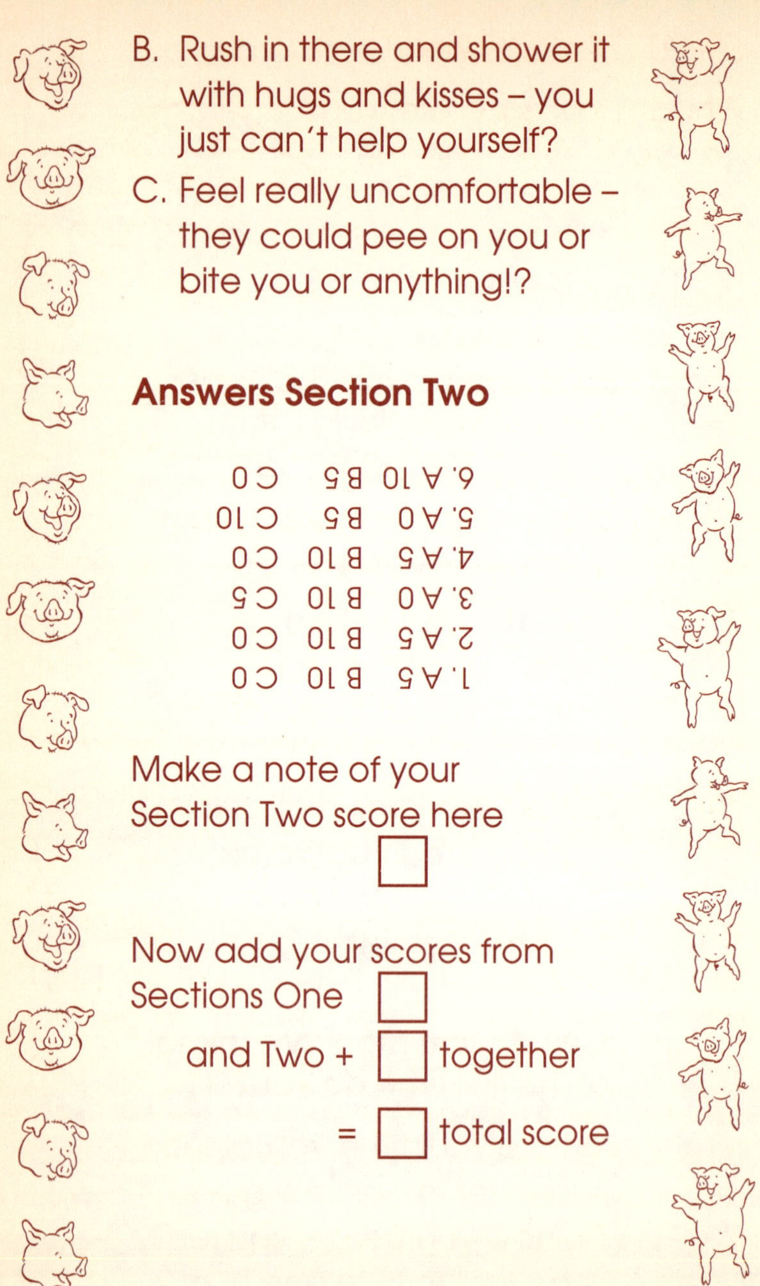

B. Rush in there and shower it with hugs and kisses – you just can't help yourself?

C. Feel really uncomfortable – they could pee on you or bite you or anything!?

Answers Section Two

1. A 5 B 10 C 0
2. A 5 B 10 C 0
3. A 0 B 10 C 5
4. A 5 B 10 C 0
5. A 0 B 5 C 10
6. A 10 B 5 C 0

Make a note of your Section Two score here ☐

Now add your scores from Sections One ☐ and Two + ☐ together

= ☐ total score

0 - 20 Total Shirker!

Whoa! How lazy are you? Do you ever get off your behind long enough to think about anyone else, let alone thinking about our friends in the animal kingdom! You're more interested about what's next on the box than what's going on right next door to you. You don't even know if any local organizations exist to help animals because you don't ever look farther than the end of your own nose. If you want to have a loving relationship with an animal you've got to give something in return. A bit of care will go a long long way and reap a whole heap of rewards. A bunny with a clean cage is much more likely to respond to a cuddle than a poor neglected bunny who's hutch is getting smelly. Think carefully before you embark on any animal-caring projects – it's not a part-time job you know. But if you shape up and give it your all, you'll be amazed how great it can be when an animal friend really shows you they're grateful.

21-75 Heart Rules Your Head!

Ahhhh! It's certainly true that you love animals to bits and that you'd do anything for them, but you do tend to be a bit of a softy and sometimes let your heart rule your head. You can't ever bear the thought of being tough with an animal, even if you know that a bit of sensible discipline can be best for the animal itself. You tend to rush in without thinking things through and let your emotions lead the way. That's fine a lot of the time, but remember, if you did help out at an animal sanctuary you might not just be seeing happy and well-adjusted animals, but also animals who've had a tough start in life – so do a bit of soul-searching beforehand and be sure you can handle it and if not, there are other ways you could help – like distributing leaflets, or working in the charity store! It's great that you love animals and you should never lose that, but channeling your love in ways that can help, practically, will make a real difference in a lot of animals' lives.

76 - 100 Animal Worker!

Wow – you've got a real sensible head on your shoulders. You know that loving animals means more than getting cuddles and cooing – it means hard work and commitment too. The best way you can show your love for any animal is by looking after it properly and if that comes to loving lots of animals, that means lots of hard work too. You've got a soft spot for all things four-legged and furry, but you're not afraid to get your hands dirty and you know that the boring, smelly jobs have to get done too. Good for you, keep going the way you're going now and I should think you'll be leaving a trail of happy critters in your wake for a long time to come.

Portrait of a . . . Pig!

A 450 pound Yorkshire sow called Den-Den was the model for a famous painting called "Pig" by James Wyeth. The painting is 5 by 7 feet in size and was first exhibited in 1971 in a museum at Chadds Ford, Pennsylvania. Den-Den was by all accounts a bit of a grump and to get her to stand still Wyeth had to soothe her by playing popular piggy tunes. He soon became very attached to her though, and many people who view the painting get the distinct feeling that Den-Den is grinning. She may well be as, soon after she began her job as artist's model, Den-Den ate seventeen tubes of paint and for the next week deposited multicolored droppings all around the Wyeth farm!

The Tall Tale of the Tamworth Two

IN January 1998 two pigs made history by winning the hearts of the entire British nation as they made a break for freedom just as they were about to find their snouts on the chopping block! Butch and Sundance (as they were later named) were two ginger-haired Tamworth pigs destined for the butcher's hook. But they were too smart for that, they took one look at the abattoir and headed for the door . . .

Tamworth pigs are a breed renowned for their versatility, intelligence, and ability to adapt to their circumstances. A hardy breed, they are able to cope quite well on their own in the wilderness, and this pair of porkers were about to prove just how well, as the long arm of the law set out to bring the fugitives to justice!

Tamworth Two Timetable

- Thursday, January 8: Arnoldo Dijulio, council road sweeper and part-time pig breeder delivers three pigs he'd reared in his back garden to Newman's slaughterhouse in Malmesbury, Wiltshire.
- Two make a break for it – wriggling through a hole beneath the encircling fence and rushing towards the gushing River Avon. They make

their brave get-away by swimming across the rushing river!

- Friday, January 9: The five-month-old pigs, worth about £50 ($80) head for Tetbury Hill where they spend a week of freedom, rooting and foraging in dense thicket nearby.
- Wednesday, January 14: TV networks, newspapers, animal groups, and the nation as a whole join the cry to save the Tamworth Two and their celebrity status grows. They've been nicknamed Butch and Sundance by now – giving Butch a bit of an identity crisis; she's a sow!
- Meanwhile, the police are on their trail. On foot, by car, and even by helicopter! The Tamworth Two become Britain's most wanted in more ways than one!
- Bidding begins in an effort to save their bacon (groan!). £15,000 (about $24,000) is the price reported when Mr. Dijulio says he will not send the pigs back to the slaughterhouse if they are finally caught, but will make sure they go to a good home – hurrah!
- Britain's tabloid press goes Tamworth Two mad, dispatching up to seven reporters

per paper to get an "exclusive" on the final capture of the red-haired rebels.

- Several close encounters of the ginger kind are reported, but although there are ten men involved in a 12-hour five-acre hunt for the pigs, they aren't brought to ground.
- Thursday, January 15: 110 pound Butch (as she's now known) is captured, loaded into a truck and rushed to a secret location.
- Pig number two (now known as Sundance) evades the law for another whole day while police and reporters stake out the area.
- Dave Lang, a 47-year-old pig breeder, has a bright idea. He takes his sow, 840 pound Samantha, to the scene where she is used as a lure for the still-missing Sundance. He's not interested though and doesn't come out of hiding. Poor Samantha goes home feeling rather rejected!
- Mary Clark discovers the perky porker snuffling among the shrubs in her two-acre garden.
- Three policemen and an RSPCA officer, watched by a huge crowd, begin a futile chase in and out of the flower-beds but still fail to pin that pig down.

- Just after 8 p.m. Sundance makes a dash for it back into the thicket. The police are defeated for another night.
- Friday, January 16: Sundance is finally captured. But he should be one happy porker as by this point he's guaranteed to spend the rest of his life in the lap of piggy luxury.
- The nation heaves a sigh of relief – ahhh! The Tamworth Two became so popular that children's picture books and soft toys of them were soon readily available. The two carrot-tops certainly put Tamworth on the map!

Happy as a Pig in Clover

In Greek mythology a man called Gryllus was changed into a pig. He was then given the power of speech and was able to have a chat with Circe (the witch that had transformed him) and Odysseus, a famous hero. Odysseus was a bit of a do-gooder and wanted Circe to restore the animals on her island to their original human form. Well, imagine his surprise when Gryllus ("grunter") said that thanks very much, but actually he'd rather stay a pig! He'd discovered through his time in a piggy's skin that he preferred the world of animals to the world of men. He said that animals were better than their human friends because they lived by natural virtues such as bravery, temperance, and general contentment, whereas everything that men did was prompted by self-interest. He was quite happy as he was and thought that being a pig was definitely much more civilized than being a smelly old man!

Buddy, the first Seeing Eye Dog

ONE of the most loving relationships ever seen between a man and his dog must be that of Buddy the German shepherd and Morris Frank, her young blind owner. Buddy was born in Switzerland at the kennels where Dorothy Harrison Eustis was training the breed for police and rescue work. When Mrs. Eustis wrote an article in 1927 about using the dogs to help blinded war veterans, she received an enquiry from Morris Frank of

Tennessee. He was invited to Switzerland to learn to work with a guide dog who would be specially trained for him. The dog chosen was a bitch called Kiss but Frank soon renamed her Buddy – the name she was to keep for the rest of her life. Frank and Buddy spent five weeks together there, learning to love each other and also how to work together as a successful team. Buddy picked up on her important job very quickly; on one walk she even dragged Morris up on to an embankment to pull him clear of a pair of runaway horses. Morris was delighted. Buddy would completely change his life from one of complete dependence on others to one of comparative freedom. Morris Frank returned to America in June 1928 and was greeted in New York by a throng of reporters who all wanted to see this "miracle" dog. They really didn't think that a dog would be clever or caring enough to cope with guiding a blind person. They were soon proved wrong as Morris and Buddy disembarked and Buddy skillfully led her friend through the heavy traffic of the street below.

Buddy became a bit of a celebrity; the public soon took Morris Frank's story to their hearts and it wasn't long before Mrs. Eustis began to arrange for the training of guide dogs to take place in the States too. In January 1929 The Seeing Eye Inc. was formed and Buddy and Morris spent much of their time touring the country raising funds for the organization so that more people could experience the wonder of having a seeing dog to guide them, just like Morris.

Buddy was quite a wonder dog and over the years she saved Morris from a number of dangerous scrapes. She pulled him away from an open elevator shaft, she woke him up when she smelled smoke, saving him from a fire that had started in the hotel they were staying in; and she even let him hang on to her tail so that she could pull him to the shore if he grew tired during a swim. Full of personality, when she and Morris would go to exclusive fund-raising receptions, Buddy could never resist helping herself to the canapés that always seemed to be just at doggy-nose height! And when she received an ovation from her audiences she always liked to give them an ovation back with some very enthusiastic barking! Morris and Buddy were devoted to each other, but more than that, they were devoted to helping others like them experience the love they had – they truly deserved each other!

Did you know...?

Wall Street in New York City got its name all because of some pesky piggies! In the early days of the city's formation the local farmers used to let their hogs roam free. Apparently they were quite an unruly bunch and the inhabitants of Manhattan Island got a bit fed up with their unrestricted wanderings so . . . they put up a wall to limit just where the pigs could roam. After a while a street was built beside the anti-piggy wall and became . . . Wall Street of course!

Parish Pig

Josephine was a tame wild boar who was bought by Albert Schweitzer, a famous humanitarian doctor. He was living and working in Africa at the time and admired his pig's wisdom in avoiding gnats at night by sneaking under the mosquito nets of one of the boys in the dormitory. Josephine was a real character and even used to attend the church services held on a Sunday, although the pastor didn't always appreciate her attendance as she tended to trail in black mud from the nearby marsh which she rolled in to cool herself down. She would then wander up and down the aisles and nuzzle up against the ladies' white skirts in her search for affection! Unfortunately Josephine never quite lost her wild streak and, when she started killing chickens, she had to be put down. A while later a visiting official heard the story of Josephine and realized it was the very boar he had bottle fed as an infant, who had been stolen. She'd never forgotten that human love and as far as humans were concerned had remained quite tame.

Albert Schweitzer has another creature to thank for the fact that he was ambidextrous (could write with both hands). He had a favorite cat called Sizi who, when he was working, was in the habit of curling up and sleeping on his right arm. He so didn't want to disturb his snoring friend that eventually he would give up and try writing with his other hand. Hey presto double handed writing skills!

The year of the Pig!

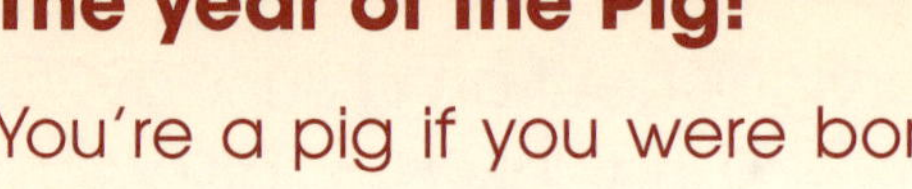

You're a pig if you were born in the following times:

January 31, 1995 to
February 18, 1996

February 13, 1983 to
February 1, 1984

January 27, 1971 to
January 15, 1972

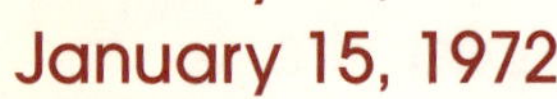

February 18, 1959 to
January 27, 1960

January 22, 1947 to
February 9, 1948

Piggy Personality

Pig people are wonderfully trustworthy, obliging, and gallant. The pig shows concern for welfare, children, and comfort. They are slow at decision-making but not indecisive. They are very intelligent.

Piggy is a country girl and likes gardening. In the home it's a contrary picture – piggy's

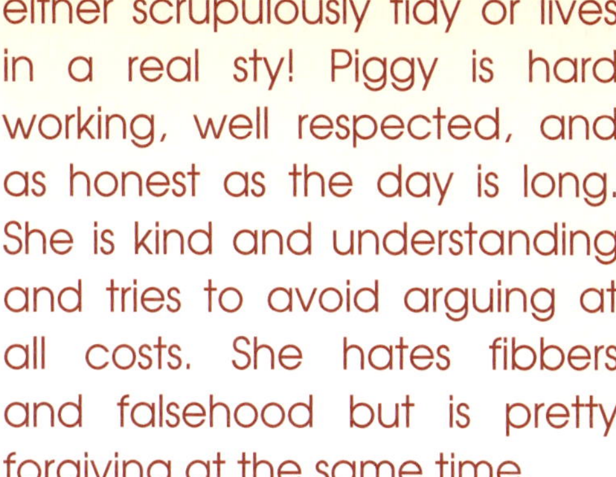

either scrupulously tidy or lives in a real sty! Piggy is hard working, well respected, and as honest as the day is long. She is kind and understanding and tries to avoid arguing at all costs. She hates fibbers and falsehood but is pretty forgiving at the same time.

Piggy Bank

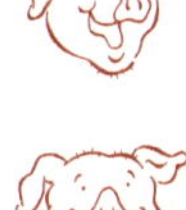

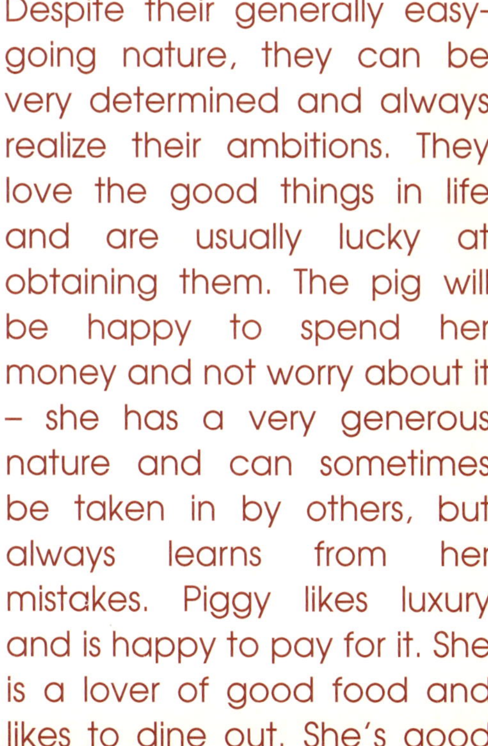

Despite their generally easy-going nature, they can be very determined and always realize their ambitions. They love the good things in life and are usually lucky at obtaining them. The pig will be happy to spend her money and not worry about it – she has a very generous nature and can sometimes be taken in by others, but always learns from her mistakes. Piggy likes luxury and is happy to pay for it. She is a lover of good food and likes to dine out. She's good

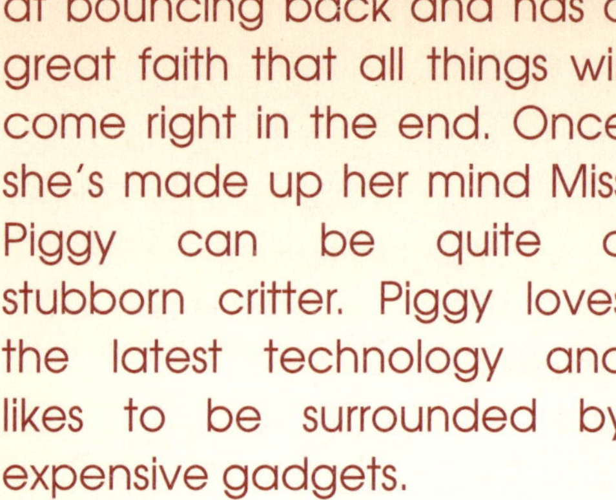

at bouncing back and has a great faith that all things will come right in the end. Once she's made up her mind Miss Piggy can be quite a stubborn critter. Piggy loves the latest technology and likes to be surrounded by expensive gadgets.

Piggy Pals

Piggy is social but prefers intimate gatherings with a few chosen friends to parties of hundreds. Piggy is a popular character and will have lots of girl and boyfriends! Pigs can get along with almost anyone, but the Snake will rub good-natured pigs the wrong way with his seriously snaky behavior. A pig is a great friend to have as she will be quite happy to go out of her way for others.

A pig's best friend will be a gallant goat!

Piggy Plans

Pig people make excellent fund-raisers as they like to work hard – especially when it's for a good cause.

Piggy Elements

1947	1959	1971
Fire	Earth	Metal
Energetic	Contented	Pushy
Pig-headed	Friendly	Energetic
Sensual	Sociable	Outgoing

1983	1995
Water	Wood
Persuasive	Good-hearted
Peaceful	Devious
Perceptive	Subtle

Piggy Personalities

Woody Allen, Ernest Hemingway, Albert Schweitzer, Elton John, Emma Thompson, Luciano Pavarotti, Hillary Clinton, Glenn Close, Henry Ford, The Duchess of York, Stephen Spielberg, Maria Callas, Cézanne, Alfred Hitchcock.

Did you know...?

Pigs don't sweat! So the phrase "I'm sweating like a pig" is a load of old hogwash! That's why piggies like a cold roll in the mud on a hot day – it cools them right down!

Who said that...?

"No man should be allowed to be President who does not understand hogs."

Harry S Truman (33rd President of the United States 1945-52)

Royal Rascals

Queen Victoria, Great Britain's longest-ruling monarch was potty about puppies. She favored King Charles spaniels (named after one of her relatives!) and had one particularly special pooch called Dash. The dog had actually been given to her mother, the Duchess of Kent, in 1833, but 13-year-old

Victoria found the dog irresistible and soon adopted him as her own. She rather liked dressing poor Dash up and was particularly fond of putting him in a pair of blue trousers and a red jacket. Victoria became queen when she was only 18 and she noted that "dear Dashy" really loved the garden at Buckingham palace. After her coronation ceremony, which lasted five grueling hours, the young queen returned to the Palace, gathered her skirts and ran upstairs to give her beloved dog a bath! When Dash died in 1840 the queen was terribly upset and had him buried in Windsor Park. Beneath a marble effigy the inscription reads: "READER If you would be beloved and regretted, profit by the example of DASH." No, I don't know what it means either! Victoria's dogs went on to win lots of prizes at the world-famous Crufts dog show. But then again if you were organizing Crufts and the queen entered her dog in the competition you might let her win too!

Presidential Pets

HERBERT Hoover's success in the 1928 presidential elections was often believed to be down to his dog, King Tut! King Tut was an ex police dog which the president got in 1917 when helping to organize war relief in Belgium. A photograph circulating during the presidential campaign showed Hoover holding the dog and smiling, and it was felt this really helped win public support by showing just what a warm and caring person Hoover really was – despite his rather brusque public manner! King Tut never lost his police training and spent his time patrolling the White House grounds checking the fences and gates. He fetched the president's newspaper during the day and if Hoover was outdoors, King Tut sat on the sections that had been read to keep them from blowing away!

Blessed Pussy Cat

The Muslim prophet Mohammed had a very beloved cat called Meuzza. One day, Meuzza was cuddled up next to the prophet having a lovely snooze when Mohammed was called to prayers. Part of his robe was caught under the cat, and rather than wake him, he cut off his sleeve! When Meuzza finally woke up he arched his back in a delighted stretch. Mohammed stroked his cat three times, making sure that Meuzza would have a permanent place in Islamic

Paradise and granting all cats everywhere the rather wonderful ability to always land on their feet – ahhh!

Presidential pets

Abraham Lincoln - On the death of his pig

"THAT pig was my companion (at age 6), I played with him, I taught him tricks. We used to play hide and seek. I can see his little face now peeping around the corner of the house to see whether I was coming after him. After a while he got too heavy for me to carry him around, and then he followed me everywhere – to the barn, the plowed ground, the woods. Many a day I have spent in the woods brushing the leaves away and helping him to find the acorns and nuts.

Sometimes he would take a lazy spell and rub against my legs, and stop in front of me, and lie down before me, and say in a language which I understood: 'Abe, why don't you carry me like you used to do?'

There was talk about the house of the hog being fat enough to kill. At the table I heard my father say he was going to kill the hog the next day. My heart got as heavy as lead.

The next morning I slipped out and took my pet with me to the forest. When Father found out, he yelled as loud as he could, 'You, Abe, you, Abe, fetch back that hog!' The louder he called, the farther and faster we went, till we were out of the hearing of his voice. We stayed in the woods till night.

On returning I was severely scolded. After a restless night, I arose early and went to get my pig for another day's hiding, but found that Father had arisen before me and fastened my pet in the pen. I knew then that all hope was gone. I did not eat any breakfast, but started for the woods. I had not gone far when I heard the pig squeal, and knowing what it meant, I ran as fast as I could to get away from the sound.

Being quite hungry, at noon I started for home. Reaching the edge of the clearing, I saw the hog, dressed, hanging from a pole, and I began to blubber. I could not stand it, and went back into the woods again, where I found some nuts that stayed my appetite till night, when I returned home. They never could get me to take a bit of the meat. It made me sad and sick to even look at it.

The next morning I saw the red place on the ground where the throat had been cut with the knife, and taking a chip, I scraped the blood and the hair that had been scattered, into a pile, and burned it up. Then I found some soft dirt, which I carried in the folds of my shirt, and scattered it over the ground to cover up every trace of the killing of my pet.

The dirt did not do its job very well, for to this day, my heart goes back to that pet pig . . . "

Pampered Pooches

Poochy pals with more money than sense can buy their doggies the top of the range in designer doggie outfits from Burberry of Piccadilly – makers of raincoats for the rich

and famous. The classic Burberry Trenchcoat has now been manufactured for dogs, to bring all that is essentially English to the poshest pooches in town. Oh yeah and it'll only cost you around $300/£185 to get your paws on one – yikes!

Popular Piggies

Between 1965 and 1971 Arnold Ziffel was the most famous pig on American TV. He starred in a popular series called "Green Acres" alongside an elegant starlet of the time, Eva Gabor. Arnold was one smart pig. He could collect letters from the mail box, pull a little wagon, sip soda through a straw, and play the piano! He was, in fact, a prize-winning pig, as he won the American Humane Association's Patsy Award for performing animals. His popularity grew and grew and soon there were Arnold Ziffel fan clubs right around the country. A group of school children from Ohio even wrote to him promising to stop eating pork chops! Sadly for Arnold he got a bit too porky for his own good and when he put on too much weight he had to leave the show for pastures new and let Arnold II take his place. But, no one could ever replace him in the hearts of the American people.

Pampered Pussycats

Dr. William Grier of San Diego was determined to make sure that his beloved cats were well looked after even after he wasn't around to see it. Hellcat and Brownie, his two 15-year-old cats were left nearly $415,000 in the early 1960s. That was, and is, an awful lot of money but then again, they did have to share it! Whereas Charlie Chan – a white cat – got to keep his $250,000 inheritance all to himself! Hmmm, I wonder how much fish you could buy with $250,000?!

Royal Rascals

King James I of England was a bit of a practical joker. But when he put a frog down the Earl of Pembroke's neck he didn't know that he was going to get as good as he gave. The Earl got his revenge by putting a piggy in the king's bedroom! What a right royal rascal!

Tales from an Inner City Farm

HACKNEY City Farm sits on a 1½ acre site in the heart of London's East End. Formed from the shell of a disused brewery it now houses a number of outbuildings for the animals as well as a café and a craft and gift shop.

As a city farm it serves a very important purpose, as many of the people (both children and adults) who visit the farm have never seen a farm animal in the flesh before. For example, one lady was amazed at just how "woolly" sheep are. When the manager jokingly told her that these were actually special sheep who'd been grazing on Astroturf, so they were 50 percent rayon, the lady was very impressed. So much so that the manager couldn't work out if she'd realized he was joking or not! It would be very sad indeed for people to go through life with no contact with animals at all and city farms are just one of the ways of ensuring this doesn't happen.

The first thing you notice when you walk in off the busy Hackney Road is the lovely country atmosphere: various ducks waddle around the courtyard and the unmistakable aroma of the pigsty wafts over. There are lots of different types of ducks most of which are quite domesticated varieties such as Aylesbury ducks; these ducks can't fly, their fat bodies being too much for their wings to carry, and they're more than happy to root around the farmyard quacking as they go. The only ducks at the farm that can fly are the pied Muscovy ducks, their gray and white coloring marking them out from their friends. And although they sometimes fly off to sit on top of the nearby old hospital building they always come back when it's dinnertime! Some of the ducks can get through to the grazing pasture by slipping through the gaps in the gate, but those that are too wide have to wait for the gate to be opened. There's great excitement when someone comes to push open the gate and let them race through. A crowd of waddly, fluffy bottoms disappears through to the field as soon as the gate is pushed wide.

The day at the city farm always starts with the 8.30 a.m. feed. They have a variety of

sheep and goats, two calves, a number of pigs, and a vast assortment of chickens, geese, and ducks. All the animals are reliant on the people that care for them, including the pet section that has rabbits and chinchillas for soft stroking time, which need cleaning out regularly. The staff at the city farm are dedicated to providing a real experience for the people that come in to see the animals as well as running an efficient working farm. They work long hours and rarely take time off: after all, animals don't stop needing to be fed and watered just because it's Christmas day!

One of the highlights of the year at the farm is the day of pig and sheep racing. The pigs have to get in training a few weeks before the big day. Pigs are very clever animals and they learn to run around the course to get to the trough at the other end where they'll find a tasty snack. Pigs are particularly partial to apples it seems. Five pigs set off at a hot trot, then the winner doesn't enter the next race and so on until there are two pigs left in the running, then the fastest three have a sudden death round – the 1998 proud winner was none other than Hyde Pork a rather attractive 4-month-old saddle-back pig who stormed round the course like a piggy possessed.

Many people have found great pleasure in the farm and its gardens. One particular family found it a very special place indeed. Next door to the farm was, until its recent closure, the Queen Elizabeth Children's hospital. In the hospital a little girl lay dying of leukemia. Her mother and grandmother would make constant visits to be by her side. They would find a little peace and solace in the farm garden before making their journey home after seeing their child. The grandmother eventually wrote telling Freya's story to the people at the farm with a donation for the garden and now, if you want a bit of peace and quiet in the garden you can go and sit in Freya's seat.

And that's not the only thing in the garden: hedgehogs are constantly found, snuffling their way through fallen leaves, and when the garden was being landscaped two other animals made their mark. The concrete had just been poured and was being left to harden when Sage, the inquisitive cat and a friendly duck decided to investigate. With every step they took a little paw and webbed footprint was left to indelibly mark the pathway so that now there's a distinct cat and duck path to follow if you wish to do so!

If you would like more information or to send a donation to Hackney City Farm their address is: Hackney City Farm, 1a Goldsmiths Row, London, E2 8QA, England. Telephone: 0171 729 6381

Presidential Pets

Did you know that even the very first president of the United States had a cat? Actually his wife, the first First Lady, Martha Washington, kept cats at Mount Vernon (their home) and even had special doors fitted so that they could get in and out unaided!

Did you know...?

Christmas time is always top for TV. And in Germany – where pork is just about top of the list of favorite dishes – the Christmas 1998 top viewing was for . . . Babe! The little pig with the big heart. Over nine million people tuned in. That's one popular pig!

Woolly Pully

One Welsh lady is a bit of a softy for her pet sheep Rambo. Despite his name, it seems the old fellow's not quite as tough as he used to be and so his owner, who lives in a

bungalow near Prestatyn, North Wales has knitted him a couple of woolly sweaters to help him keep out the chill. The 17-year-old lives in the grounds of her house and probably feels very cosy indeed!

Dearly Departed

A DJ from Essex in England was heartbroken when some thieves stole his speakers. Gary Martin, 24, didn't actually care about the speakers very much, it was what was inside one of them that he was worried about. When his beloved pooch Tyson passed away, Gary had him cremated and kept his ashes inside one of the speakers. That way Tyson would be near him nearly all of the time. Poor Gary could always replace the speakers but there was no way he could ever replace Tyson.

Nellie on the telly!

Nellie, a domesticated white Vietnamese pot-bellied pig, has appeared on America's Donahue Show twice and won the $10,000 prize on America's Funniest People with her amazing array of stunts and tricks. She can perform over 70 of them, including skateboarding and playing soccer! What an amazing pig!

Ferrety Friends

According to *Modern Ferret* magazine, babies and ferrets can be the best of friends. If you let your ferret become familiar with your new baby and introduce them to one another slowly over months, they'll soon learn to get along just fine. But you do have to watch out for your ferret trying to nip your baby's toes and . . . for your baby wanting to put the ferret in his mouth – mmm tasty!

Never Too Old to Care

A 92-year-old woman was finally rewarded for her love of animals after over forty years work on their behalf! Mary Weightman of Bedlington in North East England had spent a lifetime in the devoted care of animals when she was awarded an MBE presented by Prince Charles in 1998.

It was a very proud day for Mrs. Weightman who still works hard at the clinic she founded way back in 1954! The clinic called PAWS (People's Animal Welfare Service) was run from her home initially – luckily for Mary her husband was a very tolerant man! Eventually, Mary managed to raise the money to build a new clinic which still runs, dependent on donations and fund-raising, and until 1997 Mrs. Weightman was still among the helpers shaking a collecting tin.

But Mary wouldn't have had it any other way; she loves animals and the love she's got back from them over all those years has definitely made all the hard work well worth it!

Popular Piggies

Miss Piggy

Miss Piggy is a multi-talented, karate-chopping mega-star and femme fatale of the world famous Muppet Show.

Miss Piggy is obsessed with hot-frog Kermit who's constantly trying to fight off her amorous advances. I bet you didn't know that Miss Piggy's voice is done by . . . shock, horror . . . a Man!!! The same man in fact that does the voice of Yoda the Jedi master in the Star Wars films – spooky!

Did you know...?

The ancient Chinese regarded pigs as excellent guardians of children. Now I like the sound of that – a porcine baby-sitter – cool!

Good Dog!

Lorenzo Abundiz has his dog Cinder to thank for his good health today. When Lorenzo had a heart attack it was Cinder's actions that saved his life. As he lay on the floor unable to move Cinder ran to fetch the phone so that he could dial for help. Way to go doggy!

Owl Power

An animal carer from Kent in England was at a loss as to how to mend a frightened owl's broken wing. It was after his Christmas dinner that he had some inspiration. He took the leftover turkey ribs and made a perfect makeshift splint!

All Right Now

Conservationists who really care about animals are responsible for the fantastic comeback of our rarest breed of whale. The number of Right whales left in the whole world in the 1970s was as little as 3,000. Sadly they had been hunted to the brink of extinction.

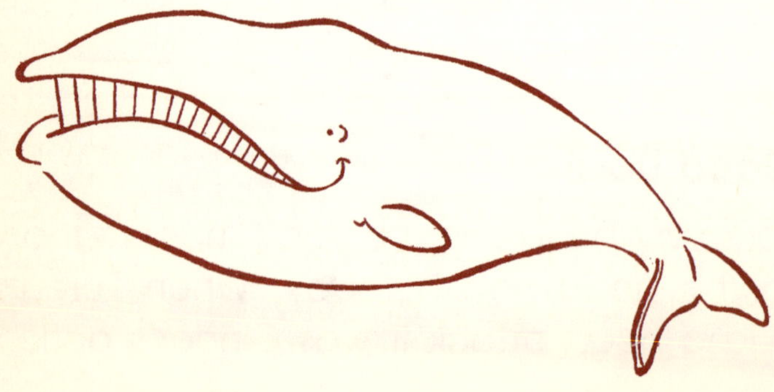

But thanks to the efforts of caring people all over the world, there are now over 2,500 in just one place – the Gulf of San José off Argentina – where 20 years ago there were only 360. Hurray for the Right whales – let's hope things keep going right for them!

Police Pig

OFFICER Ferris, a New Jersey cop, is one of the best at sniffing out illegal drugs. Maybe this wouldn't be so amazing . . . only Officer Ferris is a pot-bellied pig!

But the New Jersey cops aren't the only ones to have enlisted the services of a piggy helper. In West Germany, Louise the pig had the privileged position of sniffing out illicit substances. She was very good at her job and a popular and respected member of the force. But in 1985 the powers that be decided that Louise didn't quite portray the sort of image they wanted their police force to have, so they decided to give her the sack. What they hadn't allowed for was the upset this would cause, not just in the local community, but nationwide too! At first local dockers went on strike and then the

German Green Party got wind of the glib way Louise had been treated and petitioned for her reinstatement. Local residents wrote to the papers and soon the nationals had picked the story up and Louise was a heroine – representing repressed workers everywhere! There was nothing the police authorities could do but give Louise her job back! What a boost for workers' rights!

Pussy-cat Pig

An animal sanctuary in South Wales has a very peculiar pig. It's a pig with a bit of an identity crisis – you see, it seems to think it's a cat! It lives with the cats, shares their litter tray and at the end of a hard day curls up with them beside the warm fire . . . purrrr-fect for a piggy!

Popular Piggies

Pumbaa from The Lion King

Pumbaa the warthog is a bit clumsy and a bit dense, but he's ever so loyal, lovely, and warm-hearted and that's what counts. Pumbaa is ready to trust anyone – even a confirmed meat-eater like Simba. In the wild these clever creatures usually make use of burrows that other animals have bothered to dig out – hey, why do it yourself . . .? Warthogs are, well, warty! And they have great big tusks but to another warthog – they look gorgeous!

Cross Cat

When Sandy Forester went to Battersea Dogs Home in London to find herself a fluffy companion, little did she realize her heart would be stolen by a complete thug! Sylvester the cat had been branded the most dangerous cat in Britain as he would bite and scratch anyone that got in his way. Not only that, but he destroyed any toys he was given and no piece of furniture was safe while he was around. And at 14lb Sylvester was no lightweight!

But love can do amazing things and since Sandy's come on the scene it seems she might be achieving things five previous owners failed to do. Sylvester was such a handful that none of the previous people who tried to adopt him could cope. But with Sandy, he just might have met his match. Poor old Sylvester had found himself winding up in Battersea after he was spotted wandering the streets and looking a little worse for wear. Normally the charity can find a new home for a cat in about a month but Sylvester proved a bit more of a challenge. Even some of the staff from the center tried to look after him, but he was just too much trouble.

Now it seems that he's getting another chance with Sandy. Sandy took one look at Sylvester and something just clicked. She sees him as a free spirit – a bit like herself – and her approach of just leaving him to it seems to be working! Apparently Sandy hasn't been scratched in weeks. It just shows you what a little love can do!

Snake Charmer

SOME people will do anything for their animals and Sarah Beales is one of those people. In her late twenties, she lives, breathes, and sleeps reptiles. She runs the Proteus Reptile Rescue and Sanctuary in Birmingham, England and, basically, reptiles are her life.

Her love of reptiles started when she was just a little girl. She thought lizards were amazing and snakes were great but knew that there was no point in asking for one as her dad would be scared to let them in the house! Instead she got a terrapin and she soon realized that looking after the little critter was more work than people thought. It was when she was 18 that she and her then boyfriend wrote a letter to a local paper warning people of the perils of looking after terrapins. It seemed everyone was surprised that they didn't stay little forever and that they actually needed quite a lot of looking after. And then, to Sarah's surprise the calls came flooding in. People who couldn't cope with their scaly pets thought they had found an instant new home for them. And Sarah didn't have the heart to say no – if only for the sake of the animals . . . within months she had 57 terrapins! She was still living at home, so her poor old dad had to be very understanding!

Eventually Sarah realized that she couldn't

go on like that and so she decided to set up the sanctuary where she could care for any unwanted reptiles properly. She works from 7 a.m. to 8 p.m., feeding, cleaning, and generally caring for her animals. She has everything from Red-Eared terrapins to Burmese pythons. She's even got an 11-year-old alligator that she rescued from someone's bedroom! It's a sad fact that people are often drawn to reptiles as pets because they're a bit different. But because they're different they have very different needs and anyone who wants to look after a snake or a lizard needs to be very sure of being able to meet all those needs before taking the animal on. Luckily for alligators like Amy, Sarah's around to pick up the pieces when things go wrong.

Sarah loves her animals so much she can hardly bear to be away from them. She

never takes a holiday and only goes out twice a year – at Christmas and on her birthday. She prefers to stay in with her scaly friends or study . . . reptiles of course. In fact, she's so keen to provide her gang of assorted lizards, snakes, and terrapins the total care they deserve that she's even planning to train as a vet! And when she finally does leave the sanctuary at the end of the day, it's only to go upstairs and spend some time with her two favorite dogs!

Did you know...?

Archaeologists think that evidence of pigs indicates a settled community as pigs were difficult to herd and move over long distances.

Snort the Hero

Deborah and Collin Stople wouldn't have made it through the night if it hadn't been

for their beloved pot-bellied pig, Snort. In 1995 they were touring in their mobile home and had checked into a trailer park in Colorado for the night. They switched off the lights and settled down to sleep. In the early hours of the morning, they were awoken by the terrible squealings of Snort the pig. Deborah dragged herself out of bed to see what the problem was and to try and get the pig to go outside so that she could get back to sleep, but Snort refused to budge. Eventually Deborah gave up and headed back to the sack only to find her husband gasping for breath. It was then that Deborah realized she too wasn't feeling so good. She rushed from the trailer and raised help to get her husband out. It seemed the heater outlet on their mobile home wasn't working properly and lethal carbon monoxide gas hadn't been allowed to escape. The gas was seeping silently into the trailer while they slept and if it hadn't been for Snort they wouldn't have woken up to see another day. Snort the pig had saved their lives! The proud pig later received an American Humane Association award for her bravery.

Did you know...?

In the UK, if you own a pig and want to take it for walkies you need to get a special pig-walking licence from the Ministry of Agriculture . . . now trot on!

Badger Respect

PENNY Little has a best friend. His name is Wilf and he's a badger! Penny worked as a volunteer at a wildlife hospital when Wilf turned up in a very poor state. He was only four months old and was so small and malnourished that the vets that saw him weren't even sure if he would live. But they fought against the odds to save him and somehow he survived. Then, after two days of care he went back with Penny to her cottage in Oxfordshire where she often looked after recovering animals until they were well enough to return to their natural habitats.

Penny, who used to work in an office, now runs an orphanage for abandoned animals called Little Foxes. She cares deeply about all her charges and has looked after everything from baby birds to tiny sleepy hedgehogs who haven't managed to find anywhere safe to hibernate in time for winter. She's even had the odd duck splashing around in her bathtub! But because the animals Penny looks after aren't domestic types, they're not really suitable for keeping as pets and Penny would never dream of doing so. She's there to provide a bridge for them back to their woodland homes.

But poor old Wilf looked as if he would never be going back. He couldn't walk properly and wouldn't be able to cope on his own in the wild. But the question was, what could Jenny do with him? Really, there was only one thing for it – she'd have to keep him herself and look after him as one of her own. It wasn't difficult to love Wilf as he waddled around her small cottage and after a few weeks the usually anxious Wilf was even relaxed enough to want to play, and Jenny was more than happy to oblige him.

Wilf's a big fan of honey and loves nothing better than curling up on the sofa with Jenny for a bit of a cuddle. He can't see very well and he still has difficulty

walking but he's a really happy chappy with a very fulfilled life. He comes when his name is called and has his own special place in the kitchen where he likes to snuggle up on his blankets with his old battered teddy. He'll even have the odd sniff at the other animals in the shelter and loves teasing Penny's two Old English sheepdogs, who, fortunately for Wilf, take it all in their stride. Penny has completely changed Wilf's life; from a hopeless case to a happy, loving existence. But in return, she's got more love and devotion from one little fellow than most people could hope for in a lifetime.

Donations to Little Foxes can be sent to Cobb Hall Cottage, Back Way, Great Haseley, Oxfordshire, England, OX44 7JS.

Did you know...?

If it's a particularly sunny summer, pig farmers have to be sure to get themselves down to the store and stock up on suntan lotion – not for themselves . . . but for their pigs! Piggies' pale skin is particularly sensitive to the sun's harmful rays. Mmmm, a coconut-smelling piggy – sounds lovely!

Peaches – a Much-Loved Pig

SHARON Black had never considered herself an impulsive person until the day she fell in love with a pot-bellied pig! It was 1996 and she'd been doing some reading around the subject of being a pot-bellied pig owner and had very much taken to the idea. She persuaded her somewhat skeptical husband to drive her over to Oklahoma City and a date with fate was set.

When she arrived at the house that had three pigs for sale, Sharon knew she wasn't going to leave without one . . . they were all so cute. And when she looked at Peaches, the only girl in the bunch, she knew she was the one.

Peaches was amazing: she picked up on things so quickly. She was completely house-trained within a few days and soon figured out that the fridge door was the best one to learn how to open! She could get at it with her snout and it soon became clear that anything openable was going to have to be fitted with child-proof locks for as long as Peaches was around!

Peaches and Sharon have a wonderful time together. As long as Peaches is rested and well fed she's as happy as anything.

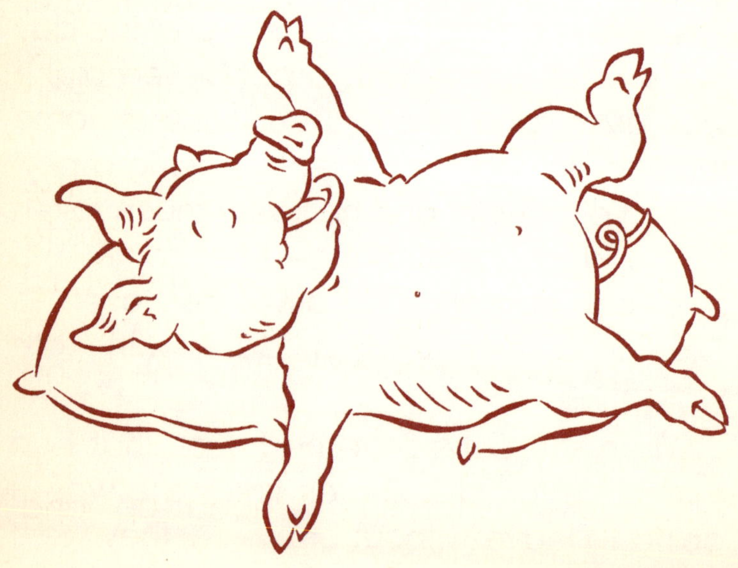

She loves the pillows on Sharon's couch and if one of them happens to be on the floor she runs up and grabs it with her snout and tosses it up in the air. Then, when it lands on the floor she falls over on it and plays dead; she rolls her eyes up in her head and becomes totally still . . . until someone laughs, then she jumps straight back up and starts the whole routine all over again. She'll keep doing it for ages and ages and then, as soon as she's had enough, she lies down and has a nap.

Sharon says Peaches is very much like a child and she even hires babysitters for her as there's just too much mischief she could get up to while Sharon's out. She follows Sharon from room to room, curls up to watch TV with her and even sleeps in Sharon's bed!

One day when Sharon had to leave the house in an emergency, she put Peaches to bed and drew the blinds hoping she would think it was night time and take a quick nap but when Sharon returned home she found Peaches, in the middle of the floor . . . "sobbing!" Peaches was so glad to see Sharon back that she jumped up and smothered her in piggy-love!

Peaches loves her weekly bath and her favorite snacks for special times are white seedless grapes and apple juice and . . . Pepsi – but only if she manages to get her snout on someone's open can and slurp it down really fast before she gets caught!

Sharon says that Peaches has brought so much joy to her life that she can't even put it into words. There is never a dull moment with Peaches around and their relationship is a perfect partnership as Peaches only gives back the love she gets given by having a very special place in a very special household.

If you'd like to learn more about Peaches antics you can look up her website on http://www.quantumportal.com/peaches

Royal Rascals

King George V of Great Britain had a pet parrot who was one of his biggest pals. He was so fond of his pet that he used to take it down to breakfast with him. He'd even let it have a little stroll over the table and nibble at the breakfast treats! Unfortunately for the other diners the parrot was a little lacking in manners and after a particularly large

serving it left a little "deposit" on the table. This, not surprisingly, got right on the queen's nerves so clever old George used to move the mustard pot over the bird's droppings before the queen got to see it. Fortunately for him the queen wasn't too keen on mustard with her breakfast!

Yoshi's Yard

YOSHI the pig lives with Knox Bronson and his wife in Oakland, California, and is a bit of an old tyrant! He's always asking for treats and if he feels he's not getting enough attention or not getting it quickly enough, he snuffles right over and plants his wet nose firmly on the nearest leg! This usually leaves a nice clear muddy noseprint from where he's spent his mornings rooting around in the Bronsons' yard!

One day though, Yoshi took it a little too far. He wanted a treat, but he'd already been quite spoiled and so he kept getting shooed out of the house and told to behave himself. Being a stubborn boar, he'd go straight out and dig up a poor defenseless thyme plant that sat on the far side of the house. He seemed to leave all the other herbs alone, but always took out his annoyance on the thyme. He'd then go straight back in and stick his freshly-muddied nose right on the first leg he came to.

After the fifth time he'd dug up the plant, Knox and his wife had had enough. Knox found a large terracotta flower pot about a foot and a half tall and planted the thyme in that. Apparently Yoshi had quite a tough time trying to work out how to dig up a plant that was in a pot that was even taller than he was!

Well, Yoshi, that'll teach you to be such a pesky pig!

To find out more about Yoshi's antics you can visit his website at: www.yoshi-the-pig.com

Did you know...?

The most money ever paid for a pig was for a crossbreed barrow named Bud. He was owned by a fellow called Jeffrey Roemisch of Hermleigh, Texas, and bought by E. A. "Bud" Olson and Phil Bonzio on March 5, 1985 for an incredible $56,000. That's one pricey pig!

Comfy Cows

A dairy farmer in Sonoma County, California, sure wants his cows to be happy. He's invested $25,000 on special mattresses for his 250 cows to sleep on at night! It keeps his cows cosy and clean and means that they are happy and relaxed and ready to deliver gallons of milk!

Historic Pigs

Some nutty medieval French people put a pig on trial accusing her of killing a baby. Poor piggy didn't win the case and was publicly hanged in Falaise, Normandy, in 1386. The French were really quite keen on trying pigs for killing children at the time and the defence counsel for the accused animals was paid for out of the public purse. Basically if you fancied bumping off an unsuspecting infant you only had to say "the pig did it" and you'd get off scot-free!

Seal of Affection

WHEN Charlene Cambourn of Cleethorpes in Lincolnshire, UK, went seal watching with her boyfriend and young son, she had no idea that she was about to put her life in serious danger. She had even less idea that it was the seals who would eventually save her life.

Charlene, boyfriend Chris and six-year-old Brogan set off one day in late January to the East coast of England for a breath of fresh air and a bit of seal watching. The trouble is, they were so engrossed in watching the lovely little creatures that they didn't notice the tide creeping in all around them, until the sand bank they were standing on was completely encircled by the icy waters of the North Sea. Night was falling and a thick fog was rolling in off the sea and it soon became clear that they could no longer really see their way back over to dry land. Chris bravely struck out for shore with Brogan on his shoulders as Charlene attempted to swim across and raise the alarm on the other side. But there was a strong tide in the area and no sooner had Charlene struck out for shore when she felt herself being dragged by the water, away from the coast, and out towards the open sea. Charlene, a strong swimmer, just couldn't fight the currents, she felt herself being pulled under by the freezing water when suddenly . . . a pod of friendly seals appeared, blocking her way forward and stopping her drifting farther out to sea.

They gathered around her and barked their encouragement. They were close enough for Charlene to touch and Charlene found herself talking to them to take her mind off her terrible situation. There were six gray seals in total and they kept in a

tight circle around the swimmer until lifeboats eventually came to her rescue over an hour later. Exhausted and freezing Charlene was rushed straight to hospital, but when she was released the next day there was only one thing she could think about. The caring gray seals that saved her life.

Precious Piggy

Ben the pig is the much loved friend of Maria Hennesey who runs a Sanctuary for Injured Animals in Gwent, Wales. He's such a popular porker that he even has his own fan club. He lives in a little brick house and eats

delicious vegetarian dishes which are served to him with his favorite drink – strawberry milkshake. What a lucky pig!

Lucy the Wonder Pig

KATHLEEN Plauche is the president of NAPPA (the North American Pot-bellied Pig Association). She's a real pig-aholic and has had lots of wonderful experiences with her piggy pals.

One particular pig called Lucy had a very loving nature. She loved to go to schools and shows and meet lots of different people. She also liked to pay a visit to a certain nursing home where she would perform a number of tricks to keep the elderly people that stayed there amused.

She would even be taken round by Kathleen on a tour of the rooms, visiting people who were too weak or unwell to make the move into the living room to see her.

Lucy was very popular, she really brightened the residents' lives, and she seemed to understand too that she was doing something special. Then one day when Kathleen took Lucy to visit, a new lady had moved into the home. She had been there about three weeks but seemed to be having a lot of trouble settling in. She seemed very unhappy and refused to speak to anybody. She sat in her wheelchair day in day out, or lay on her bed staring straight ahead and barely moving. Everybody was very worried about her, she didn't even respond when her family came to see her – it was as if she had given up on life. Then . . . she met Lucy!

Lucy was ready and waiting in the living room, when somebody wheeled in the old lady in her wheelchair. As usual the lady stared straight ahead, seeming not to notice anything that was going on around her. She didn't even notice Lucy. But Lucy noticed her and she seemed to realize that all was not well. Acting on her instinct Lucy

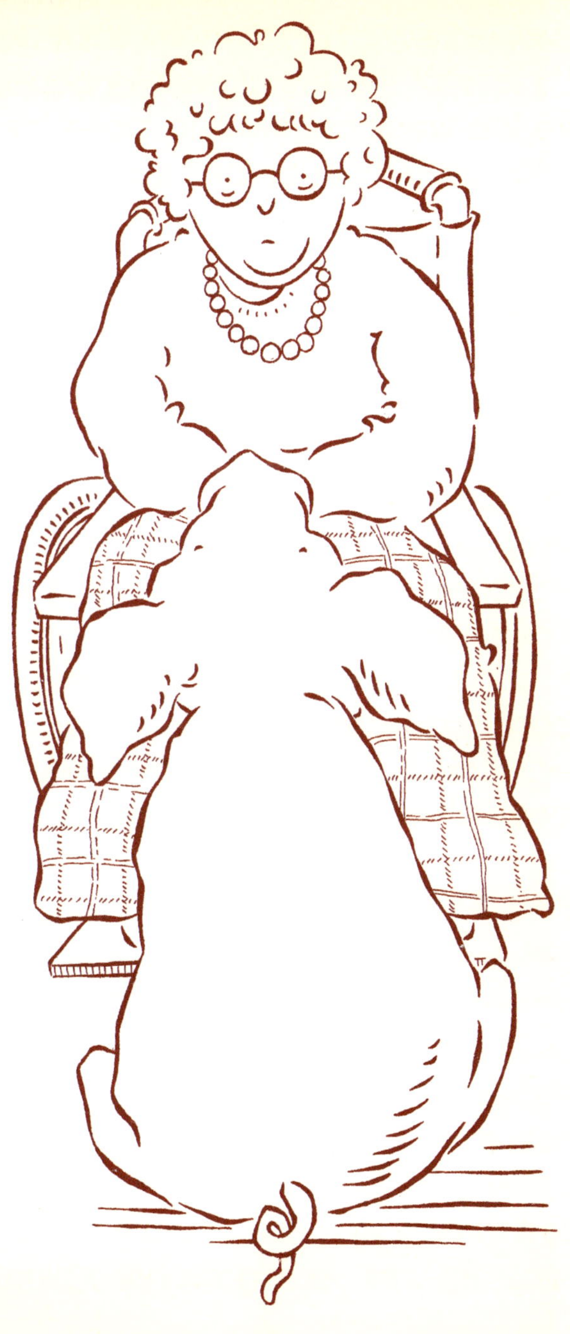

trotted straight over to the lady and laid her head in her lap. Lucy then nudged the lady gently on her folded hands. The lady slowly looked down at Lucy and began to smile. Not a shy smile but an excited happy smile. She then said the first thing she'd said in three weeks: "Look! A Pig! I had a pig when I was a little girl. She was my pet and I loved her more than anything!"

Everybody was delighted. They'd spent weeks doing everything they could possibly think of to lift the old lady out of her gloom but nothing had worked. And then she met Lucy and all her sadness seemed to just disappear. And from that day forth, she was a changed person. Her happy memories had brought her some happiness in the present and now that she had a story to tell she was willing to chat away with her fellow residents for hours on end. And whenever Lucy came to visit she would of course save a special moment to be petted by her new friend.

Kathleen is a great one for taking her pigs to shows all over North America. She has won all kinds of prizes including winning the prestigious Grand Champion Boar ribbon more than once! Once Kathleen was taking some pigs to a show in Oklahoma.

Sometimes her pigs need to fly as the show is so far away, but this time she decided they could drive and got the station wagon ready to take four baby pigs to the show in Oklahoma city. It was quite an eventful journey as whenever they stopped, people got very excited to see four happy pigs riding along in a station wagon!

Eventually they reached Oklahoma City late in the evening and booked into a motel room. Kathleen loved her little piggies so much that she just didn't think she could bear to leave them alone in the station wagon over night, so she decided to sneak them into the room where she was staying with her partner Terry. They'd brought a couple of play pens with them so the pigs would be safely enclosed while still having a bit of space to play in. Pot-bellied Pigs are very clever and can pick up toilet training in a jiffy – so that wasn't a problem either! They just had to hope their piggy pals would keep quiet and not alert anyone to the fact that they were inside their room, as Kathleen was quite sure the motel owner wouldn't be too pleased about that!

The next morning all was well. Kathleen and Terry got up very early so that they could sneak out again without anybody seeing their additional guests. Terry decided to play with the pigs. The trouble was, one pig got a little over excited and the next thing Terry new it was squealing away for all it was worth! They managed to settle the pig down again and Kathleen went off for a shower while Terry headed across the courtyard to get a cup of coffee. He soon came rushing back to the room though! The whole place was crawling with police, a person in a room nearby had called them saying they thought someone must be having a fight there was such a commotion!

Kathleen and Terry only just managed to get away with it – sneaking the little pigs back out before anybody caught them. Which just goes to show what can happen when you love your pigs so much you can hardly bear to leave them. And after that one little piglet got a new name . . . Screamer! And it really suited him too!

If you would like more information on pot-bellied pigs you can contact the North American Pot-bellied Pig Association via their web site at: **www.petpigs.com/nappa.htm**

Pony Pal

A pony called Ant won the hearts of the locals where he lived in Blaenavon in Gwent, Wales. He'd started life as a pit pony, working with the men down in the mines, pulling coal wagons up and down tracks deep underground. He worked at Blaenavon colliery for 24 years and when he retired he kept his link with the colliery by being bought by an ex-miner, Philip Davies, who then owned a pub. Ant had a very nice retirement; Philip looked after him very well, giving him the run of the field next to the pub and feeding him three square meals a day each accompanied with a delicious pint of beer! Ant had other fans

too. His field was right next to a local bus stop and people waiting for the bus couldn't resist taking the time to stroke and talk to the little pony. He arrived in his field in 1966 and stayed there until his death in 1978. Hundreds of cards and flowers were sent in memory of the gentle old pony who had enriched so many people's lives. But there's something to be said for the love he got, as at 40, Ant was the oldest pit pony ever to have lived. Ahhh!

Milking Time

Milking Time at Mark Purdey's farm in Exmoor is quite a sight to behold. The farmer claims to increase his yield by playing the flute and the saxophone to his 70-strong herd of jersey cows. Apparently the girls find the flute very relaxing while the bull is more of a sax fan. He'd better be careful what he plays or he could end up with a milk-shake-rattle and roll – groan!

For the Love of Iris

SCOTT Gurney has a very special friend – Iris the pig! Every morning he greets her with his "Iris the Pig Song" – "Iris is a big fat pig, a big fat pig, a big fat pig. Iris is a big fat pig, she loves her 'belly rubs'!" And she does, but being a 95lb piggy she has to have her breakfast first of course!

Iris was born on March 11, 1994; she is a pot-bellied pig who is black all over with little white socks and a white streak running down one side of her neck – apparently inherited from her mother. She didn't come into Scott's life until 1997 though, but since meeting her, he's never looked back. Iris had been adopted by a couple in Canada but the husband developed a rare pig allergy and had to find a new home for the poor pig. They got in touch with Nancy Shephard who has a large farm in central Missouri and is a well-known piggy person and it was there that Scott met the pig of his dreams. Despite his fiancée, Laura, wanting a dog, Scott decided that Iris just had to be theirs!

He got a second opinion though, from his mother – she wanted him to get a dog too! But, when they pulled up at Nancy's farm for a second time on a cool rainy day only one pig was standing waiting for them, with her tail wagging like crazy and Iris's fate was sealed!

Iris is one loved-up pig. She lies on the floor next to Scott with her head squashed between the two pillows he's lying on and gets a head-to-toe rub'n'scratch which makes her sigh with pleasure. She used to sleep in the bed with Scott some nights – before he got married! – and Scott soon learned how the expression to "hog the bed" came about. When pigs sleep together in nature, they try to get maximum heat from each other by sleeping belly to belly. The trouble was, when Iris tried to do that, Scott usually ended up with a big trotter right in the stomach! Pigs are hot critters and hairy – so sleeping with Iris was like having a big scratchy hot-water bottle. And when Scott got too hot and tried to move over, even by just an inch, Iris would just huff and shuffle right over back beside him again. By the morning Scott would be clinging to the last few inches of bed hoping not to fall out altogether!

Iris is a big fan of Scott's piano playing. She likes soft comforting tunes and will lie sleeping next to the piano with her side against it as he plays her a soothing lullaby. In fact, Iris likes to follow Scott around wherever he is in the house and keep an eye on what he's doing and nothing makes him happier than to come through the door after a hard day at work to see Iris smiling in the doorway and wagging her tail. He comes in and sits on the sofa, and before he can even get his shoes untied Iris is already there, flopped at his feet, and waiting for her belly rub! And in two minutes . . . Iris is fast asleep! Ahhhh!

If you'd like to see a picture of Iris and find out more about her lovely life you can do so through the NAPPA web site at: **www.petpigs.com/nappa.htm**

A kiss for Kimmie

A fifteen-year-old boy from Scunthorpe took his first aid training very seriously. It was a good job too as he was soon called upon to save a life . . . the life of his five-month-old hamster, Kimmie. In May 1996 Matthew Cook found poor little Kimmie lying deathly still on the floor of his cage. Without pausing for thought Matthew went straight into resuscitation mode and gave his hamster the kiss of life. As for Kimmie, well, after all the excitement he thought it was time for a bit of a snooze!

Royal Rascals

Edward VIII was another royal with a devoted doggy. His dog was a pug and the dog slept happily on the king's bed every night. Then one night, the little dog seemed to change his mind for no reason at all. He slipped off the bed and lay down beside it to sleep on the floor. That night, Edward died. It seems his pug was psychic!

Prize Piggy

One little piggy was lucky as lucky could be. He was up as first prize in a Hungarian lottery

– which wasn't very lucky as he was probably going to end up as someone's Sunday dinner. But, Liz Kaernestam of Austria, heard about the lottery and was so upset at the thought of the little piglet's imminent fate that she bought every single ticket in the lottery. Luckily for her and the pig (if not that surprisingly) she won! And now this little piggy lives happily ever after in its new Austrian home!

Pig in a Pond

PRISCILLA the Pig from Houston, Texas, loved a little paddle in Lake Somerville near where she lived. Her owner Victoria Herbert had given her swimming lessons and her piggy paddle was quite a sight to see. One day when she was having her usual dip in the lake she heard the cries of a young boy in distress. Eleven-year-old Anthony Melton had got out of his depth and was treading water madly trying to keep his head above water.

Priscilla didn't give it a second's thought; she started to pig paddle furiously across to the boy and, using her snout, helped to keep him above water until he finally managed to grab hold of her collar and let her drag him to shore.

Priscilla won an American Humane Society award for her bravery but, even better than that, had an entire day named after her! August 25, 1984 was proclaimed "Priscilla the Pig" day by the mayor of Houston. What an honor!

Road Sense

The Great British philosophy of being nice to animals has recently extended to badgers. A special underpass has been constructed under one of their busiest roads, the M5. It's only a foot wide and is there to save plodding little badgers from the perils overhead. But it's not just the Brits who can't bear the thought of any animals getting squidged! The Swiss have run a large bit of major road near Zurich underground so that Hares can hop happily across it above ground.

Lucky Duckies!

A TOP-NOTCH hotel in Memphis, Tennessee, isn't just home to paying guests, but . . . to a family of ducks too! Daisy, Daphne, Denise, Daffy, and Donald live in the lap of luxury at the Peabody Hotel and nobody thinks they're quackers! The mallards have the posh penthouse suite all to themselves and have regular feasts provided by room service. With anything from grain to cabbage to crunchy carrots on the menu, these ducks really do want for nothing.

Daisy and Co. are the latest in a long line of Peabody Hotel ducks. The trend started over fifty years ago when the then-manager thought the lobby fountain would look a lot nicer with a bit of additional wildlife! So he bought a few ducks and the rest is history!

The lobby ducks were such a popular addition to the hotel that they've stayed ever since. They've even been on travel programs and are quite an added attraction for people staying there. The ducks start their day at 7 a.m. with an elevator ride down to the lobby; they then waddle along the carpet, accompanied by

a couple of bellboys, before taking the plunge and dipping into the clear soothing waters of the glamorous marble fountain that is the center-piece of the lobby. They then spend the rest of the day swimming around at their leisure and delighting anyone who happens to be passing.

The ducks even get time off for good behavior with carefully timed vacations on a farm outside Memphis. While they're away they do a house swap and the farm ducks get to have a few weeks of luxury in their place at the beautiful Peabody Hotel!

History Pigs

In Celtic times the boar was regarded as a sacred and prophetic beast. Druids at the time actually called themselves "boars" as they wanted to be so closely related with the magical pig. And Nordic warriors added boars' tusks to their helmets to help them be as strong as a swine in battle.

Nice-one Nanny!

A goat called Sarah was so loved that her owner decided to make sure that Sarah would have a happy life even when he wasn't around to see to it. Sarah inherited a whacking $115,000 from her owner's estate.

Royal Rascals

Charles I of England was convinced his pet black cat brought him good luck and he carried it everywhere with him. When the cat died, Charles was very worried that this was a bad omen and he feared that his life would never be the same. He thought all his luck had just up and left him. Actually he wasn't wrong – the next day he was arrested and his beheading followed shortly afterwards. To make up for the lack of his lucky cat Charles I took his poor doggy to his execution instead – yuk!

Pig Quiz

Just how much do you know about your porky pals? Are you a total boar-brain or pure pig-headed? Find out in this pig-tastic quiz for porky-philes everywhere!

1. Who said:

A. That'll do pig?

B. Th-th-th-th-that's all folks?

C. La la laaa, la la laaa, la la laaa la laaa?

2. What was the name of the hero-pig in E. B. White's book *Charlotte's Web*?

3. What breed were the two pigs that escaped the chop in Malmesbury in Wiltshire in 1998?

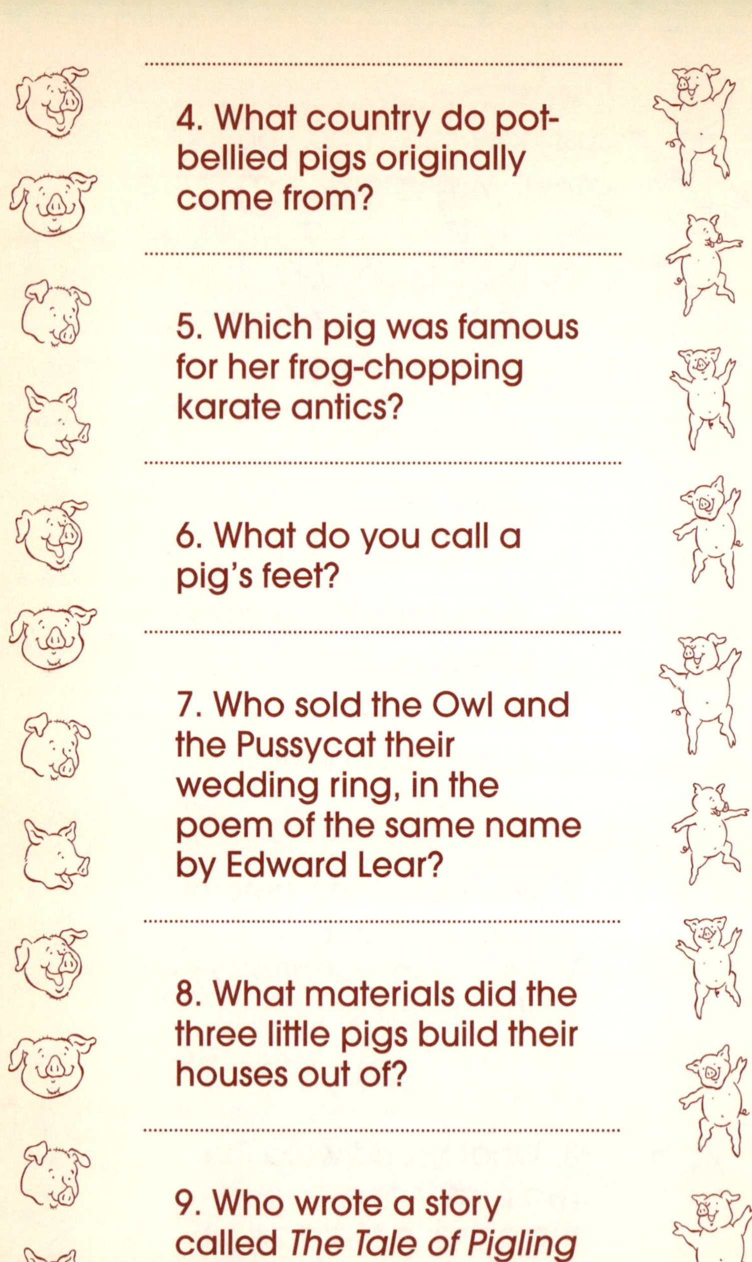

4. What country do pot-bellied pigs originally come from?

5. Which pig was famous for her frog-chopping karate antics?

6. What do you call a pig's feet?

7. Who sold the Owl and the Pussycat their wedding ring, in the poem of the same name by Edward Lear?

8. What materials did the three little pigs build their houses out of?

9. Who wrote a story called *The Tale of Pigling Bland*?

10. What would you be doing if you were driving your pigs to market?

11. What was a pig-wife?

A. A woman who married a pig?

B. A female pig?

C. A woman who sold crockery?

12. What's a pig in a poke?

A. A pig in a small space being poked?

B. A pig playing a round of poker?

C. A gift or purchase that you didn't see before getting?

13. What sort of person would you be if you were pig-headed?

A. Very good looking?

B. Very ugly?

C. Very stubborn or obstinate?

14. What's a pig's whisper?

A. A very quiet grunt?

B. A short space of time?

15. What does the saying "it'll happen when pigs fly" mean?

16. Which book has a very bossy pig called Napoleon in it?

Answers

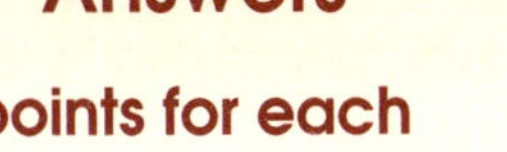

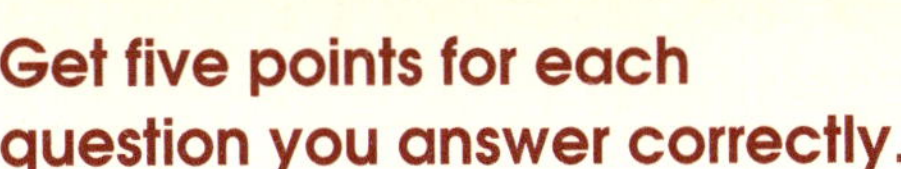

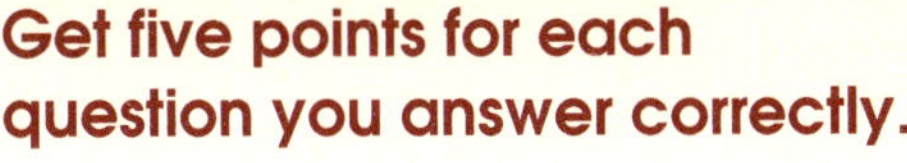

Get five points for each question you answer correctly.

1. A. Farmer Hogget in Dick King-Smith's *Babe – The Sheep Pig*
   B. Porky Pig
   C. Babe
2. Wilbur
3. Tamworth
4. Vietnam
5. Miss Piggy
6. Its trotters
7. A piggy-wig*
8. Straw, sticks and bricks (5 points per item)
9. Beatrix Potter
10. Snoring very loudly!
11. A. 0 B. 0 C. 5**
12. A. 0 B. 0 C. 5***
13. A. 0 B. 0 C. 5
14. A. 0 B. 5
15. It'll never happen!
16. *Animal Farm* by George Orwell

*The owl and the pussycat wanted to get married but didn't have a ring. They met a Piggy-wig in a wood who had a ring in the end of his nose and they said *"Dear Pig, are you willing to sell for one shilling, your ring?" Said the Piggy, "I will."*

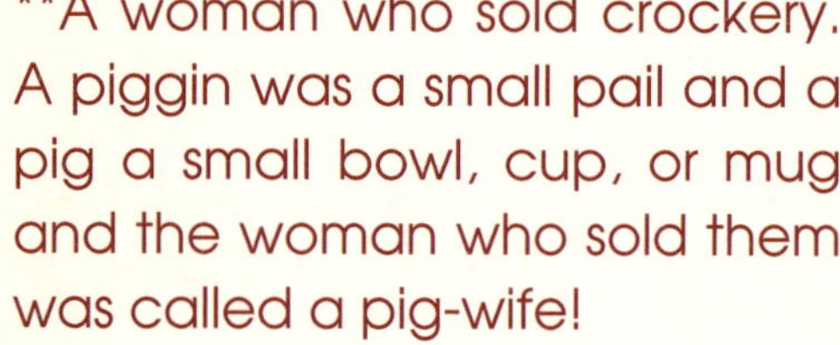

**A woman who sold crockery. A piggin was a small pail and a pig a small bowl, cup, or mug and the woman who sold them was called a pig-wife!

***A gift or purchase that you didn't see before getting it. This saying comes from a trick of days gone by when a trickster would try to fool some innocent into buying a pig which he had in a sack – he would say he couldn't open the sack to let them see as the pig would run away. When the poor innocent got the "bargain" home and opened the bag, out would run ... a cat! Hence also the saying "letting the cat out of the bag."

Scoreboar-d

0-35

So, you may not know all there is to know about things pink, squealy and porcine, but look at it this way – the only way is up!

36-70

Not bad! You've got a trotter in the door and with a bit of revision you could up that score in no time. You're about half way on the old oink-ometre – so good for you!

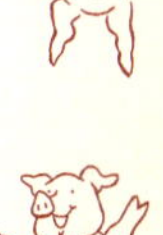

71-100

Wow! Your head is full of hogs, packed full of pigs, and swimming with swine – and that's no hogwash! Great going – you're a true blue pig-headed piggy pal! Congratulations!

Rent-a-Rhino

What do you do if your house is too small for a pet, your sister's allergic to all things furry, and your dad's scared of spiders . . .? Easy, adopt a pet! Lots of zoos around the world let you take your pick, from their aviary to their ape houses. At London Zoo you can choose from over 100 species. Costs range from £20 ($32) for a sleepy dormouse to £6,000 ($9,600) for a great big elephant. And if you're really strapped for cash you can club together with your friends and adopt a bit each! For just £30 ($48) you could be the proud owner of one fifth of a boa constrictor or a third of a darling little bush baby. Some famous people who probably don't have too much time at home to dedicate to a pet have even adopted one – Tina Turner for example has forked out for an Asian lion at London Zoo – I expect she liked their matching hairstyles!

For London Zoo contact: Adopt an Animal, London Zoo, Regents Park, London NW1 4RY (0171 449 6262).

Did you know...?

The runt of the litter, if adopted as a pet pig, is known as a St Anthony's Pig!

Dogged Dedication

IT'S true, the British are soccer crazy. They'll follow their teams through thick and thin, crying when they lose and cheering when they win. But one of the most dedicated fans in the whole country is . . . a dog called Honey. Honey the Lurcher was chosen by Eric Maddison when he went to a rescue center to find a dog. The staff warned him that the dog was terrified of men, but Eric had fallen so in love with her that he thought he could win her over. And he could! So much so that he takes her with him to watch the match whenever he goes to see his team, Scarborough, play. Soccer supporting, though opening up to women, is a predominantly male pastime, so Eric has worked quite a miracle to get a dog who was terrified of men to come and sit with a

whole bunch of them for over ninety minutes, without a squeak.

From a sad start in life, having been beaten and abandoned by a previous owner, Honey's made a remarkable comeback. She's so popular at the pitch that she's now even got her own Scarborough FC membership card and every week she's proud to wear a scarf and coat in the team's red and white colors, provided by Eric's wife. Honey's found a new life of security, soccer, and love!

Greedy Pig

The heaviest hog on record was a Poland China pig called "Big Bill" who was owned by a man called Burford Butler of Jackson, Tennessee in 1933. He measured 9 feet long and weighed 2,552 pounds. He was such an incredible porker that his tummy actually touched the ground!

Here's Looking At You . . .

CARING vet Paul Evans has made a very big difference in a little owl's life. Boris the Siberian eagle owl is a very special fellow; he's only one of 10 of his kind in captivity and as such he's very important. There are only 100 breeding pairs of Siberian eagle owls left in the wild and Russian conservationists are very keen to use the few fellows in captivity to breed more baby owls which can then be released back into the wild and ideally, in time, start having little owl families themselves and bringing their species back up to full strength. The problem for poor Boris was that Siberian eagle owls rely heavily on their sight for mating and Boris was blind. Until Paul Evans came along that is. Boris, who lives at the Screech Owl Sanctuary in Truro, Cornwall, has now had his sight completely restored. Boris had cataracts, a common complaint in humans and animals that usually takes a simple operation to fix. But they're quite rare in birds and although Paul Evans had performed lots of cataract operations on cats and dogs before, he'd never done one on an owl! Boris had to wear a special little gown and have an anaesthetic before Evans made a tiny cut in Boris's eye and then used a hollow needle to suck the cataracts out. Boris, who had his operation in January 1999, is now as good as new and looking forward to meeting his first lady love! And Paul Evans can be as proud as any vet could be to know that not only did his work save Boris' sight, but it could have helped along the way to saving a whole species too!

Smells Swine

If your piggy gets a bit stinky, here's what to do: Follow in the footsteps of the clever keepers down at Marwell Zoo near Winchester, England. When their porkers got a bit more whiffy than normal they called on the services of some top aromatherapists who came and gave the piggies a quick once over with their yummy smelling oils. The result – some very sweet smelling swine with a stress factor of zero!

Did you know...?

If you wanted a pint of beer in a London pub you might ask for a pint of pig's!? In Cockney rhyming slang a "pig's ear" = beer!

Royal Rascals

The Scottish monarch, Mary Queen of Scots, had a very devoted doggy. Poor Mary was to be beheaded and her little dog trailed her to the spot where her execution was to take place, hiding under her long petticoats. After the dreadful deed was done the dog ran out from under and lay down in the space between the dead queen's head and her body. Poor poochy.

Afterword

Obviously we love piggies for all the right reasons – they're intelligent, loving, and full of fun. But sadly, both in the US and the UK there is a growing problem with people buying pigs as pets (particularly pot-bellied pigs) and then finding that they're rather more of a handful than they'd imagined and abandoning them or having to hand them over to sanctuaries and other charitable animal care organizations. So, the thing to learn from this is that yes, pigs are lovely animals and can make wonderful pets but, and it's a very big but, only if the people who take them on are willing to provide the time, energy, environment, resources, and love that these clever creatures require – not to mention the cost of their upkeep. So, if you want to be a real piggy pal don't ever get one as a pet unless you know you can give your pig the best life possible, for the whole of its life!

Did you know...?

Did you know...?

Did you know...?

Did you know...?

Did you know...?

Did you know...?

Did you know...?

Did you know...?

Did you know...?

Did you know...?

Did you know...?

If you know any amazing stories about pet pals or wild animals (especially bears!), why not send them to the author who would be delighted to read them:

Kate Tym
c/o Element Children's Books
The Old School House
Bell Street
Shaftesbury
Dorset
SP7 8BP

E-mail: Kate.Tym@btinternet.com